praise for

ONE CHOICE
CAN CHANGE YOUR LIFE

"This book is a fascinating and moving account, marked by a striking insider's view of prison life. Harvin Moore has written a vivid, compelling portrayal of the good – and the not-so-good – in American corporate culture, and how he came to terms with the not-so-good."

> – WILLIAM HOPPER
> Co-author of *The Puritan Gift,*
> A *Financial Times* Top 10 Business Book of the Year

"*One Choice Can Change Your Life* is a powerful, moving book that grabs you by the collar and puts you in touch with what is really important in life."

> – BRIAN TRACY
> Author of *The Psychology of Selling* and *The Art of Closing the Sale;*
> World renowned sales and success expert

"With this painful memoir of his progression from respected Houston lawyer to prison inmate, Harvin Moore shows how his attempts to save a failing business crossed the line into fraud. He did it knowingly, with fake transactions that seemed harmless at the time, but which would send him to jail. *One Choice Can Change Your Life* provides a good lesson to anyone tempted to make a similar choice."

> – DANIEL FISHER
> Senior Editor, *Forbes* Magazine

"This amazing book is not just about business. It's about the intersection of business, life, personality, passion, and integrity. And it's a book we all need. Harvin presents a handbook for marketplace integrity, following your calling, and recovering from even the most extreme setbacks. If you have ever wondered how to succeed in business—while keeping your integrity—then read this book!"

– Ed Rush
Author of *Fighter Pilot Performance for Business*
Speaker and former Marine Corps Fighter Pilot

"If you're ready to jumpstart your life and business, then read and absorb the information in *One Choice Can Change Your Life*. Harvin is a true inspiration, with a heart full of serving and giving to others!"

– James Malinchak
Co-author of *Chicken Soup for the College Soul* and
Two time College Speaker of the Year
Founder, www.BigMoneySpeaker.com

"In an economic climate of distrust and corporate scandal, *One Choice Can Change Your Life* confirms that the future of business belongs to those who create organizations based on trust and integrity. Harvin Moore's inspiring book brilliantly combines business strategy, tales of corporate success and failure, and a personal story of ultimate redemption. Every business leader who seeks significance should read this book."

– Larry Broughton
Author of *Leadership Lessons From A Former Green Beret*,
Founder and CEO, Broughton Hospitality
and 2009 Ernst & Young Entrepreneur of the Year

ONE CHOICE

CAN CHANGE YOUR LIFE

How A Top Business Leader

Lost Everything

But Found His True Calling

HARVIN C. MOORE III

VindingMark
PUBLISHING CO.

ISBN: 978-1-61712-123-4

Library of Congress Catalog Card Number: Available

Cover designs by Birdsong Creative, Inc. | www.birdsongcreative.com
Edited by Phil Newman

Printed in the United States of America

Vinding Mark Publishing Company, LLC
14027 Memorial Drive, #346
Houston, Texas 77079

This book is dedicated to my wife, Mary I. Jensen,
who provided a spark of light in an ever-darkening cave,
and joined me in the journey through what turned
out to be not a cave but a tunnel, with a new
life waiting at the other end.

Contents

Note to Reader

If you are struggling with a decision and feel pressured or tempted to make the choice that satisfies the temptation or mitigates the pressure, this book will force you to stop and think about the consequences of such a choice.

As a result of the collapse of the energy, real-estate and banking industries in Texas, and particularly in Houston during the 1980s, under extreme pressures, I made some wrong choices which changed my life forever. I was convicted of bank fraud, sent to prison and lost everything. In the process, I caused a great deal of embarrassment and suffering to my family, friends and employees which I cannot ever undo.

As I left for prison, I was encouraged to chronicle the experience so I could write about it upon my release. I kept a daily journal and mailed it home each day so that during the guards' random locker searches, they would not find and confiscate it.

Soon after my release, I began to write the account that you now hold in your hands. But because of some disheartening comments I received at a writing conference, I lost my confidence to continue.

Nevertheless, each year I received more and more invitations to speak about my experiences. Throughout fifteen years of sharing my story at business seminars, conventions and retreats throughout the United States, Canada and the United Kingdom, I was often told, "You should write a book!"

I heard in those encouraging voices a keen interest in knowing more about what I had gone through, and why I was now able to stand before them and confess these most intimate and painful memories.

To write this book, I had to "dig up the bones" and honestly relive what I had endured. In doing so, the stress I had once survived resurfaced and intensified as I analyzed, dissected and disclosed for public consumption my experiences. Most people would not want to do that because it is too personal and involves others who were dealing with their own pressures; but I knew in my heart that I must reveal my entire journey to make it complete and truthful. So I continued because I knew there were so many who could benefit from this book.

The business chapters may be too detailed for you, but please know that describing several large, complex business operations and transactions was essential in order to understand the pressures that I felt.

I have described my prison experience and what it was like in as much stark detail as possible. I was there to be punished. I am not a victim, and I am not bitter about all that occurred.

To protect the identity of the inmates, I have used only their first names, and I have changed the names of inmates' spouses. All other names are correct, as are the facts, to the best of my knowledge.

If you think what happened to me could never happen to you, it is my hope and belief that after reading this book you will understand how, under pressure or temptation, you, too, might rationalize to justify a fateful decision.

And it is my deepest desire that my story will motivate and empower you to make the right choice.

ONE CHOICE
CAN CHANGE YOUR LIFE

Prologue

I drove slowly through the barren, forbidding terrain, cresting a small rise only to see another one just ahead, always the same, yet leading toward something inevitable, something alien to everything I had ever known. After a number of these undulations, a slow-motion roller coaster ride, we came to the end of the road. I stopped the car and stepped out into the frigid air.

Standing in the open, glancing uneasily and quickly in all directions, I saw little movement other than fallen leaves and bits of paper tumbling along the ground. The sky was heavy with clouds; they cascaded off the distant mountains to my left and then rolled quickly toward me, gathering darkness as they approached, pushed by a strong wind. It was the middle of the day but seemed much later. A solitary, barren tree struggled to exist next to the one-story stucco building. The air felt damp even though in the few steps I had taken my shoes were covered with dust. Tiny bits of sleet-like gravel stung my face. The cold wind penetrated my shirt like a blue norther blasting through a barbed-wire fence. I shook uncontrollably.

A man appeared and stopped six feet from me. I noticed his polished black boots, sharply creased gray pants, black battle jacket, dark complexion and high cheekbones, reflective glasses and coarse black hair. My gaze moved down the man and lingered on the glint of silvery metal attached to his black patent-leather belt. Looking more closely, I noticed it was a set of handcuffs. I shuddered involuntarily.

Glancing over my shoulder, I was reassured to see Mary standing there by the car, holding my coat, watching silently, sadly. Then, I saw a tear slide down her cheek.

We had driven onto the Fort Bliss Army Base at El Paso, Texas. Following instructions from the MP at the gate, we had taken the Sgt. Simms Road through the part of the fort known as Biggs Air Field, to its end where we would find the Federal Prison Camp.

It was noon on Friday, January 3, 1992.

At every critical moment in our lives, we make a choice. The choice is influenced by our families, environment and experiences. It is shaped by pressures and temptations which reflect our fears and our hopes. In the end, the choice leads to a result—often an unintended one. When it is revealed, we stand alone…and reflect on why it all happened that way.

" We make choices every day,
but we don't ever choose the result.
The result flows from those choices,
so if we make a bad choice,
we risk getting a bad result."

– HARVIN C. MOORE III

One

The Worst Day of My Life

Driving through the opening in the cyclone fence that surrounded the prison camp, the place appeared eerily deserted. I was nervous, fidgety, as no one would tell me what to expect. Now I was there.

Stopping at the main building about fifty yards from the guardhouse, I went inside to tell someone I was there to self-surrender while my fiancée, Mary, waited in the car. There was no registration desk, just a small room with a thick glass window and a prison guard standing behind it. Looking shocked to see me, he told me to go back outside, stand by my car and wait for a guard. Carefully following his orders, I walked back to the car and turned, just as a guard hurriedly walked up, stopped about six feet from me, and said, "You were supposed to stop at the guard house."

I gulped. "There was no one in it."

"Walk back over there and check in," he commanded.

I followed his instructions, then returned and faced him.

"May I keep these?" I asked, glancing down at a few clothes and books I had brought with me.

Eyeing me from behind his dark glasses, he said flatly, "No, and you need to take off your coat."

As I was complying, Mary spoke up. "Can he keep his Bible?"

"No."

Pointing at my leather shoes, he asked, "Do you have other shoes?"

"Yes, I have a pair of tennis shoes."

"Put them on. You'll be glad you did."

After changing shoes I asked, "What about the cash I brought?"

He remained stoic. "Bring it with you, and I'll put it in your account."

"My wristwatch?"

He eyed the twenty-dollar Armitron. "It's okay. Bring your driver's license and let's go."

He motioned toward a trailer behind him. My stomach tightened. I caught my breath as I saw where we were going. The time had arrived for me to face, and enter, this unknown world.

Trying not to let my eyes reveal my fear, I turned, quickly kissed Mary goodbye, and held her for a few more seconds. Then, with a pounding heart, I turned and followed the guard. I could hear her car door close and the motor come to life as she backed out and left. I didn't turn back to wave. I couldn't.

I followed the guard into a trailer labeled "Receiving and Discharging" (R&D). He pointed to the doorway on his right. "Stand in the middle of the room," he said in a serious, authoritative tone.

I walked into a small room with metal shelving on three sides. He followed me in, stood near the door facing me and said, "Take off your shirt, and fold it up."

From a metal shelf he took a flat, pre-creased cardboard sheet, folded it into a box, dropped it on the floor, and kicked it over to me. "Put your clothes in there and they'll be mailed back to your home."

After I had taken off my shirt, he said sternly, "Now take off the rest of your clothes." As he spoke he pulled out a pair of latex gloves and, with an exaggerated motion, slowly worked them over his fingers until each hand was gloved.

"Run your fingers through your hair like this," he said, demonstrating by moving his hands back and forth in his own hair. After I had done that, he said, "Now, turn around, bend over and spread 'em."

I shuddered to think of what might be next. However, he did not move toward me or touch me. He simply said "Okay" and, pointing to the shelves to my left, commanded, "Put on that pair of coveralls and come back into the other room."

I breathed a deep sigh of relief. The strip search was apparently over.

The olive-green boxer shorts and dark-blue coveralls felt cold against my skin, but I hurriedly put them on, along with a pair of flimsy white socks and my tennis shoes. He snapped my photo and took my fingerprints, then pointed to a chair for me to sit in. Next, he took my cash, prepared a receipt showing that the money was deposited into my commissary account, and put my driver's license in my prison file. Finally, he gave me some forms and told me to go over to a table and complete them.

Sitting at the table was another inmate who had just arrived. We introduced ourselves, talking in whispers. Phil lived in El Paso; he had moved there after retiring from a career in the military. When we had both completed the forms—mostly about whom to notify in case of an emergency—the guard reviewed them. Finding them acceptable, he told us to follow him out the door. Phil and I fell in several steps behind him and continued our conversation as we headed into the blustery wind, toward a warehouse where we'd be given clothing and bedding.

Inside, workers who were clearly inmates asked my sizes for pants, shirts and shoes. I was handed a blue windbreaker and baseball cap with "FPC" (Federal Prison Camp) above the bill, along with towels, sheets, a pillow case, blanket, a stack of boxer shorts, light-blue T-shirts, dark-blue pants, a blue web belt, medium blue shirts, white socks and a pair of black, steel-toed work shoes (size 13, one size too large and way too wide). Because the camp had been expanding its population rapidly, the warehouse was out of a full set of pants, quilts, winter jackets, stocking caps and gloves.

Barely able to see over our piles of clothing and bedding, Phil and I hustled to follow the guard to a barracks across the grounds, past the R&D trailer to a building labeled "Franklin." I was told it had been named for nearby mountains at the foot of the Rockies.

Walking across the barren ground, I could see a few inmates scurrying toward different buildings, but otherwise the place still looked deserted. What would the inside of Franklin be like? I wondered. I knew I would be among the oldest inmates, that the overwhelming majority would be 18 to 25 years old, and that few would be White Anglo-Saxon Protestants like me. I knew my education and business experience would have little value here. I would have to stay alert and learn the culture quickly to survive.

My heart pounded as we entered Franklin. We were led up to a second-floor office where another guard gave us small plastic bags containing a disposable razor, shaving cream, toothpaste, toothbrush and comb. Anything else would have to be purchased at the commissary. I looked down the hall and saw two aisles separating three rows of double bunks where men were sitting or standing and talking.

Suddenly, another guard bounded up the steps and hollered, "Mail call!" The inmates rushed into the hallway where Phil and I stood. Within seconds, they surrounded us. The guard began calling out names. By the tenth letter, I thought he was reading the names from the Mexico City phone book. The population of this prison was overwhelmingly Hispanic. And I didn't know more than a dozen words of Spanish!

When mail call ended, the guards took Phil to the first floor to his bunk. I was assigned one on the second floor. I noticed a communal bathroom with showers, a wall-mounted telephone, and a TV room at the far end of the hallway. My lockers were the two against the wall by the foot of my bunk, one stacked on the other. The folding metal chair lying on my mattress was also mine. "Don't lose it," the guard warned. "You won't get another one."

Just as I began to make my bed, several guards stormed in yelling, "Count time, count time!" At 4 p.m., every inmate had to stand silently at the foot of his bed to be counted. The inmate who slept in my lower bunk spoke no English, but motioned to me what to do. As I figured it out, he smiled and nodded. The first pass didn't result in the correct number, which, as I soon learned, happened often. The guards again shouted, "Count time!" and walked through. Either they got the same number or got another wrong number, so we had to be counted a third time. Once they got it right, the guard called out, "Count clear!" Immediately, most of the inmates hurried out across the grounds to the main building to line up for supper.

I turned to finish making my bed when a smiling, round-faced, prematurely white-haired inmate walked up, held out his hand and said, "I'm Clarence from the Valley." I told him my name and we shook hands. He pulled out of his pocket a half-full bottle of Head and Shoulders shampoo.

"Take this," he said. "You'll need it 'cause they didn't give you any."

"Thanks, but are you sure? I can get some at the commissary next week."

"No, you take that; they may be out. It's yours."

"Well, thanks. I'll pay you back just as soon as I can."

"No, don't do that," he said. "You just give something to the next guy who comes in. That's the way it works here. I've been down for a long time and I've still got several years to go. We'll have lots of time to talk. In the meantime, don't ask too many questions if you don't know someone real well."

"Thanks, Clarence. I appreciate the shampoo and the tip."

I sighed with relief. Clarence had given me my first insight into this sub-culture, which was better than I had feared, and had introduced me to prison vernacular. "Down" meant imprisoned.

As I put away the clothes in my locker, another man, about my height but thinner, walked up and, with a smile that would light up the darkest room, said, "I'm Max, welcome to the neighborhood!" He, too, held something in his hand—deodorant. I thanked him and said I'd pay him back, but he gave me the same response that Clarence had. Still smiling, he said, "Come on and eat supper with us."

Max radiated friendship.

"I'd love to, but can you wait just a minute while I finish putting up my stuff?"

"Sure. Can I help?"

"No, it'll take just a minute."

I shoved my clothes in my locker and closed the door. Pulling on my windbreaker and cap, I followed Max over to his bunk.

Max introduced me to several men who "lived" near his bunk: Tom from Austin, who worked at UNICOR, which ran the laundry on Fort Bliss; Bob from Albuquerque, the food-service clerk; and Sean, also from Austin, who had a different UNICOR job. Since Bob had eaten earlier (as food-service employees did,) Max, Tom, Sean and I walked across the grounds to the cafeteria.

The dining room had individual tables with four attached orange plastic seats that swiveled, just like the décor at an early McDonald's. Standing in line, I confirmed that few Anglos and even fewer blacks would be my prison mates. From our supper conversation, I realized that probably two-thirds or more of the inmates had been convicted of a drug offense.

I quickly learned it was a cafeteria only in physical layout. We had no food choices. The inmates working in food service simply filled our plate from the steam table and handed it over. Then we'd go to the beverage dispenser against the far wall and serve ourselves tea, water or Kool-Aid.

My tablemates assured me that no one would instigate a fight with me, though occasionally inmates did get in one. If they did, they'd be sent to the "hole" (solitary confinement) at La Tuna Federal Correctional Institution (FCI) at Anthony on the New Mexico-Texas Border. Then, they probably wouldn't be returned to this camp.

After supper, I hurried to the guard's office in Franklin, as instructed. As new arrivals, Phil and I were handed garbage-can-sized plastic bags and told to pick up cigarette butts and trash on the grounds, within a lighted area around the Franklin entrance so the guards could see us, and then throw the bags in the dumpster when we finished.

Within minutes, I was shivering from the cold wind penetrating my windbreaker. I used my sleeve to wipe my nose while thinking tomorrow I'd better put a paper napkin from the dining room in my pocket, and dress more warmly. I would have to pick up trash and cigarette butts until assigned a job.

After throwing my trash bag into the dumpster, I trotted back to the Franklin entrance where inmates were clustered smoking cigarettes. The distinctive smell of Mexican food wafted through the air. As I stepped into the hall, it smelled like I had walked into a Taco Bell. What was going on? Hadn't we eaten supper just a couple of hours earlier? On the second floor, several inmates were lined up outside the TV room waiting to use the small microwave oven to heat up dips, cheese and tortillas they had bought at the commissary. Evidently, they wanted more than the typical prison meal.

I climbed onto my bunk after getting paper and an envelope from the guard—they were called "hacks" by the inmates—and sat cross-legged to write to Mary. Before I had finished, the hack called me to his office. I jumped down and walked to his cubicle. He led me down the hall to a locked closet and opened it to reveal bathroom-cleaning supplies.

"Clean the bathroom," he commanded. It was the job of the newly arrived to clean them on nights and weekends. We were called "A&Os," which stood for Administration &

Organization, the group in which inmates were placed for "counting" purposes until they were assigned a job.

So now, I would not only pick up trash and cigarette butts but also clean the bathrooms until I was assigned a regular job. This was done to demean all new inmates, graphically reinforcing their lowly status. I really hoped I would get a regular job soon!

Count time occurred again at 10 p.m. Standing by our bunks was not required this time; we only had to be on or near them. The lights went out at 11 p.m. But I wasn't quite ready to fall asleep that first night.

Two

Unintended Consequences

L ying down on a lumpy, thin mattress and putting my head on the pillow—if that's what you call a striped sack filled with a handful of what felt like Styrofoam shells—my mind began going back over my career. How could I possibly be spending the night in a federal prison…as an inmate? What had gone wrong, and why?

I thought back to early 1973. My wife, Nancy, and I had agreed to buy and remodel my Aunt Faith Bybee's large, beautiful home in the prestigious River Oaks subdivision of Houston. I was in my fifth year as a partner at Bracewell and Patterson, the city's sixth-largest law firm, and was as well situated as any of my classmates. I had been president of the Junior Bar Association and had made some lucrative investments. Our children, Harvin IV, nine, and Marian, six and a half, were doing well in school. We were active in our church. Life was good, and business pressures were few and manageable. I was pleased with my marriage and career, and optimistic about the future.

Then, in October 1973, Tyler Todd, a real-estate developer and client of mine, asked me to buy out his retiring partner. After much consideration, I decided to make the investment, which required only assuming his partner's liability on their various loans. It was by far the largest investment I had ever made. That night, after signing the agreements, I had an unusual foreboding, a sinking feeling that it was a mistake.

Within a few months I learned why, as bad news starting rolling in like a rising tide—we had a cash-flow problem. In addition, various debts secured by the real estate started coming due, and the loan commitments we had to pay them off were being dishonored. This was escalating into a serious problem. I couldn't believe it had gone so bad so quickly. It was swamping me with unexpected work on top of my normal legal practice.

By the beginning of '74, I was juggling my law practice with managing a sinking real-estate business that took more and more time.

The Arab oil embargo of 1973 had resulted in a quadrupling of the price of oil overnight, from $3 a barrel to $12, which was followed by rampant inflation leading to a recession that crushed the economy by the middle of '74. Interest rates rose to a historically high 12%, and no credit was available.

By the summer of 1974, I was wearing down. I worked at the law firm from early morning until late afternoon, then went to Tyler's office and put in another four or five hours. The strain must have been noticeable to everyone, but particularly to Fentress Bracewell and the law firm's managing partner, Carlton Wilde. One afternoon in July, they walked into my office to discuss the situation. During our conversation, I finally realized the enormity of the financial obligations I had undertaken. It became clear that I could not continue to practice law. I had to devote all of my time and effort to solving my real-estate problems. They agreed to help make that transition as smooth as possible.

With their permission I would resign from the firm, and from our investment partnership, effective the end of the fiscal year (September 30, 1974)—exactly six years after I had become a partner. Because the real-estate company owed the law firm so much money, we also agreed that my interest in the firm's investment partnership would be liquidated at its current value, but paid to me on a dollar-for-dollar basis only as we were able to pay the legal fees we owed. Finally, the firm worked with me to shift my clients and various matters to other lawyers within the firm immediately so I could begin working full time with Tyler. All in all, it was a fair arrangement.

By July 1974, I was in the real-estate development business full time without intending to be—an example of questionable choices and the law of unintended consequences.

When I came home from my meeting with Fentress and Carlton, I told Nancy that we had agreed it was best for me to leave the firm and focus exclusively on resolving my real-estate problems. I had not discussed any of this with her, so the news stunned her. Her father was a lawyer, both of her grandfathers had been lawyers, and her brother, Ben, had just joined Vinson & Elkins. It's what men in her family did.

Her questions were unending. "How could you leave the firm and become a what? A real-estate developer? What's that? How are you going to make a living? Are we going to have to move after we just moved in? This is more than depressing—it's terrible!"

I countered matter-of-factly, "Nancy, I was just making another investment like I've been doing. You didn't have any complaints before when I made them, and they've been pretty darn successful."

Nevertheless, it was very clear that this was my problem and I would have to work my way out. I couldn't let the situation sink me, no matter what. But I felt terribly isolated.

If the recession didn't end soon, there would be no way to avoid bankruptcy. From childhood, my Uncle Charles Bybee, who had been chairman and CEO of Houston Bank & Trust, a large downtown bank, had preached that no honorable businessman ever took bankruptcy. Bankruptcy was a cop-out. Even though Uncle Charles had died, his attitude was ingrained in my thinking. I could not fail.

When the news of my resigning from the law firm ricocheted through family, friends and business associates, they were shocked. I tried to put a positive spin on the situation and my future. But the reality was that I was no longer a partner in Bracewell & Patterson. I felt adrift. My problems were so large and consuming that I had little time to think about my loss of identity. But in my heart I knew that I had made a foolish investment that had cost me an envied position in a growing, well-regarded law firm.

Within a few days of meeting with Fentress and Carlton, the movers arrived to take my furniture out of my large, comfortable office on the 18th floor of the First City National Bank Building. As I followed them out of the building, I said goodbye to now-former colleagues and accepted everyone's warm wishes for success.

The movers took my lawyer's desk and credenza to the offices that Tyler rented at the rear of a non-descript apartment complex near San Felipe and Loop 610. It was cramped, but the rent was cheap. There were no funds from which I could draw a salary, but fortunately, and, to her everlasting credit, my aunt generously agreed to a moratorium on our home-mortgage payments until I began receiving an income. That significantly reduced my personal expenses. I was deeply appreciative and relieved.

Within a week of my leaving the law firm, Buddy Lander (C.W. Lander), the demanding president of River Oaks Bank, one of the firm's clients for whom I had done a lot of legal work, called to ask what was happening. Buddy, nine years my senior, had a stocky build, silver hair and usually wore a navy blue suit, silk tie and French-cuffed shirt. He looked like a banker to be respected. With a large loan outstanding to Tyler and me, he was concerned. Not only had he lost his primary lawyer for the bank's loan work, but he had a large position as one of our creditors.

Disgruntled with my decision to leave the law firm, he switched the subject to how Tyler and I were going to pay back the loan. Expressing my anxiety over the precarious state of our business, he suggested I talk to the bank's chairman. Buddy sounded optimistic that such a conversation might prove helpful.

At the end of that meeting, however, the chairman said he wasn't interested in buying anything from us or investing with us. I was disappointed, but I was pursuing every idea and suggestion. I hoped Nancy could, at least, appreciate the doggedness with which I was seeking a resolution.

Several days later, John Eikenberg, a lawyer and mutual friend of Tyler's and mine, came to our office to discuss a matter he was handling for us. As he prepared to leave, he said to me, "Harvin, I don't think you ought to be doing your own legal work. You don't have the time, and it will distract you from solving your problems. So, I want y'all to just send me all your legal work and I'll take care of it."

"John, I know you're right, but we can't afford you or anyone else," I groaned.

"Don't worry about that. I know you're gonna make it, and so you don't have to pay me now. It doesn't matter if it takes a year or more. You just pay me when you can."

Tyler and I were dumbfounded by John's offer. I knew I couldn't ask anyone at my firm to represent us because we already owed them a large sum with no idea when we could pay them. John was absolutely right that I shouldn't try to represent us in anything. I had been concerned about whether we could find someone to handle our legal battles. But, out of the blue, John appeared and relieved one big problem— and lifted a tremendous amount of pressure and worry from my shoulders.

A few weeks later, I talked with another longtime friend, Jerrol Springer, who was curious why I had left the law firm. Jerrol's insurance agency wrote all of our policies, many of which we were required to have in force according to loan covenants. He had bought my cousin Joe Westerlage's insurance agency that Uncle Charles had organized for Joe a few years earlier.

After Joe had graduated from the University of Texas and moved to Houston to go into business, Uncle Charles thought Joe would do well with a general insurance agency, particularly since a number of his bank customers could be encouraged to place their insurance with Joe. However, Joe had difficulty growing his agency and struggled to service current clients. Uncle Charles encouraged Jerrol to buy it from Joe, which he did and employed Joe for a number of years.

Joe would play a role in a critical chapter of this story a few years down the road.

In my conversation with Jerrol, I admitted that we simply could not pay for our insurance coverage even though we had to have it. Without hesitation, Jerrol said, "I'll make sure you have the coverage, and you pay me back when you can."

Jerrol solved the second major problem for us and took that worry off my agenda.

I was overwhelmed by John's and Jerrol's confidence, and grateful beyond words. Their friendship and extraordinary confidence in us strengthened my own resolve to succeed. I couldn't let them down.

As 1975 began, Tyler and I formed Village Developers Inc. (VDI), to put all of our properties into one overarching corporate entity for legal and tax reasons, and executed a buy-sell agreement. But we still had sporadic cash flow. Tyler had no ability to fund anything, so to keep the doors open, I had to fund—from my savings—our payroll of seven people, including Tyler at a reduced salary, or we would have to shut the business down and file bankruptcy. Doing that would leave me with liability for all of the unpaid loans, and I would have to take personal bankruptcy as well.

By summer, all of my funds had been exhausted. With nowhere else to turn, I swallowed my pride and embarrassment and asked for help from Nancy's father, Ben H. Powell Jr., a senior vice president and general counsel of Brown & Root Inc., a subsidiary of Halliburton. (Brown & Root later became an independent company known as KBR.) Would he make a loan to me secured by our weekend place in the hill country, a rock cabin on seven acres along Cypress Creek in Wimberley? We had bought it five years earlier using the profit I made on a real-estate development that Tyler had brought to me.

After reviewing the values of comparable properties in the Wimberley area, Ben decided that instead he would have Nancy purchase the property as her separate property.

Texas is one of eight "community property" states, meaning that from the date of marriage, everything that is earned or acquired by either spouse belongs to both equally until the marriage is terminated. However, the property owned by either spouse prior to marriage can be classified as "separate property" and remain as his or her property exclusively, as long as it's not "commingled" with "community" assets. In addition, anything a spouse receives after marriage by gift or inheritance is separate property and remains such as long as it, too, is not commingled with community assets. Nancy had significant separate property at the time of our marriage. I had no idea of its value; it was hers, and her father was the manager of those assets. The message to me from the inception of our marriage was that whatever those assets were, they were not to be touched. With her purchase of the Wimberley property, it would become separate property rather than a community asset, though our family could continue to use and enjoy it.

I was relieved. I had gotten a reprieve and avoided filing bankruptcy.

I continued daily communication with our lenders but was unsuccessful in persuading even one of them to give us a new loan. Everyone was in a state of suspended animation, just waiting for the recession to end. The rejections wore down my optimism, culminating with a loan proposal to Allied Bank of Texas, a large downtown bank that held the first lien on 30 acres that we wanted to develop into Candlelight Oaks Village.

When I got home that evening, Nancy was putting dinner on the table. After we said the blessing, we discussed what had happened during Harvin's and Marian's day at River Oaks Elementary School.

Always cheerful, little Marian asked me, "Daddy, did you sell a house today?"

We did not build and sell houses, we only sold lots to homebuilders who would do that. But as they sold a house, they would buy another lot to build another house, so she got the gist, if not the exact procedure.

"No, Kutch (her nickname), no one sold a house today. Maybe tomorrow."

Then it got quiet as we ate. I replayed, over and over in my mind, Allied's decision. After a few minutes, Nancy spoke from the other end of the table.

"You look down."

"I am," I slowly responded.

"What happened?" she asked without much curiosity.

"It's a long story. I've been trying to get Candlelight Oaks Village refinanced at Allied Bank. That was especially tough because I had to explain why we had 25% fewer lots than Tyler had told them when the original loan was made. However, I finally got our loan officer to recommend it. The loan committees approved it, but then it had to go to the executive committee for final approval. All of this has taken several months. Today, he tells me it was turned down. I just can't believe it! The ones who know us and the project best approved it, but they got overruled. It's so frustrating. We really need that loan because it will solve so many problems. So," I said dejectedly, "that's why I'm down."

She looked straight at me and said very coldly, "Well, I wouldn't loan you any money either."

I stared at her in disbelief. I said her words over again in my mind. In them—and in her tone—I sensed resentment, anger, even a hint of fear, all reinforcing her detachment from me. She's saying Allied was right; that no one should lend me any money. That means the bankers, and even she, can't trust me to pay them back. I'm not to be trusted? She's on their side! I felt a dagger pierce through my ego.

After we cleaned up the kitchen, Harvin, Marian and Nancy went upstairs while I took the garbage out, opened the lid and threw it into the can as hard as I could. I had controlled my anger up to that point, but now it bubbled over. I walked down the brick driveway to the sidewalk and shut the wrought-iron gate, then began to pace rapidly up and down the driveway, talking to myself to burn off the anger and disappointment.

"I'll show her and those Allied Bank executives. I'll build a company everyone wants to do business with—so big and successful that I'll never have to guarantee another loan— bigger than anything her father has done because I wanted to show him, too. I'll survive this problem and prove to her that although she might never loan me a dime, hundreds of lenders will. My company will become a model. I'll show everyone!"

It was a defining moment in my career. Feeling more determined than ever, I walked upstairs to my office. No one in the family noticed. We handled this like we handled all the stress that came up—we didn't talk about it.

VDI's largest subdivision, Brays Village, was in the Alief area of west Houston. First City National Bank of Houston held a mortgage on the land. Our loan officer at First City, Charles Dixon, arranged for Tyler and me to present our development loan request to Fred Hohmeyer, head of the Real Estate Loan Department. Soon after the meeting started, Mr. Hohmeyer cut our presentation short by asking,

"What size are these lots, and what's their selling price?"

"Forty-five by ninety (feet), and $4,500," I responded.

With that, he stood up, harrumphed that he would never see such lot sizes or prices in his lifetime, and walked out of the room. My heart sank. Here we go again. Not another Allied situation...and this time we didn't even get past the loan officer. Our situation was desperate. If First City wouldn't make the loan, then it had to give us a working-capital loan of $250,000 or we would have to file bankruptcy. Mr. Hohmeyer's response could not be final.

Charles broke the silence by saying, "Let me keep working on it."

Several months later, First City approved our working-capital loan and a financing commitment for Brays Village. Finally I could be repaid for my advances to VDI, draw a salary, make timely mortgage payments, and VDI could pay Bracewell & Patterson, which, in turn, would pay me for my share in the firm's investment partnership. It was my best day in almost two years. There was no celebration at home that evening, but I knew Nancy was relieved.

With the economy recovering, Houston sat astride a burgeoning oil-and-gas boom. Within six months, Allied Bank made the development loan on Candlelight Oaks Village.

Two years later, in 1977, we were in a position we could only have dreamed about. Brays Village was one of the fastest-selling subdivisions in Houston, despite being the first development composed entirely of zero-lot-line houses (one wall of the home is built on one of the side lot lines). It also became a laboratory of sorts for Houston's City Planning Commission to determine appropriate building set-back lines, density and green spaces for such developments.

Nancy's father, Ben, now executive vice president of Brown & Root (B&R), was in charge of its London office, from which all of its work in the North Sea was managed. As general counsel, he still handled international contracts for the company while overseeing all the other legal matters. His schedule and work ethic would exhaust anyone even 15 years his junior. One Friday evening, he called me.

"Harvin, don't you have a big aerial map of Harris County at your office?"

"Yes sir, we do."

"Let's go out there in the morning. I want to look at it."

After we arrived at my office, he focused on a large, undeveloped area on the west side of the Beltway, a designated right-of-way for a future freeway in Harris County.

"How big is this tract?" he asked.

"About 700 acres. It's owned by the R.E. Bob Smith estate."

"What do you think it's worth?"

"Around $20,000 an acre."

He absorbed the number and suggested we take a closer look. As we drove around, he continued, "B&R's policy is to own half of the space it occupies and rent the other half, which gives us flexibility if we have to cut back. But that ratio is now more than three-fourths rental, so we need to own more of our space. The west side of Houston is ideal since so many of our employees live in this general area."

The following Thursday, Nancy and I ate dinner at the Powells'. When Ben arrived, predictably late, I mixed a gin and tonic for him. He casually mentioned that he had made a deal to buy the 700 acres. He and the other trustees of the B&R Pension Fund had voted Monday to buy it, all the documents had been prepared the next day, its New York City bank had funded the money, and the sale was consummated that afternoon.

I was taken aback. All of that in five days! I had never seen such a large real-estate deal ($14 million) get done so quickly. In my career, I had been focused on gaining access to capital, but it became clear how much more important it was to control capital. You could write the check!

As our subdivisions sold out and new opportunities arose, we bought more land to subdivide and opened our own title-insurance agency, real-estate brokerage firm and property-management company, each one giving us more vertical integration.

It was clear that VDI needed more space, and I wanted to build an office building. We bought a seven-acre tract across Bellaire Boulevard from Beltway Bank that could accommodate two buildings. Needing a financial partner for the equity, I approached Nancy's father for the first time with an investment proposal. With significant property investments in the Huntsville, Texas area, in west Texas around Pecos, and in Austin—where his father, Judge Benjamin H. Powell, had begun acquiring property decades earlier—Ben was intimately knowledgeable about real-estate investing.

I prepared the business plan and projections for our office building and presented them to him over Labor Day weekend when the family flew to Pecos for the opening of dove season on his farm (an annual tradition). By the time we returned to Houston, he had agreed to make the investment in return for 50% ownership in the building. I was elated. I took it as a vote of confidence in the project and in me.

By the summer of 1978, our Corporate Plaza One was built and completely leased. As the last lease was signed, I could hardly wait to call him and deliver the good news. Things were looking up.

In 1979, Tyler and I organized Arbor Home Corporation and began building single-family homes in Houston. We were growing our businesses and becoming a large, vertically integrated real-estate company. Amazingly, lenders began competing for our business. With that growth, we soon needed more office space and developed Corporate Plaza Two adjacent to our first building. Ben was, again, our equity investor. Upon its completion, all of our companies moved into building two. With the booming Houston economy, it was fully leased shortly after completion.

About two years after we completed Corporate Plaza Two, Travelers Insurance Company offered to buy both buildings for $12 million, provided we guaranteed the leases. Owing only $8 million on the buildings, it would be a huge profit after just a few years. I was ecstatic. With controlled excitement, I called Nancy's father and told him of the incredible, unsolicited offer.

He heard me out. Then, in a methodical, unemotional way, he began to ask questions about the proposal. I answered all of them to his satisfaction except for one: "Now, what's this about guaranteeing the leases?"

"Travelers just wants to make sure the leases presently in place will not terminate or default soon after its purchase of the buildings," I replied, thinking it a formality.

"That could be a big number," he said calmly. "It's pretty risky. Sounds like Travelers wants us to absorb the market risk for them."

"To some extent they do, but we can probably limit that as to time and/or dollars."

"Well, I don't like the idea of guaranteeing any leases to them. Besides, we'll have to pay taxes on our gain and the recapture of depreciation."

"Yes, sir," I conceded, "but if we could limit the guarantee of our rent roll for, say, one year, we would be pretty safe because we shouldn't lose any tenants in that period. We have only a few leases maturing next year, and we have prospects. I think we can limit our risk to no more than $250,000. Even if that entire amount materialized, we still would make a huge profit in a short time, with plenty of cash to pay the taxes."

"You know," he replied, "what we have here in these buildings is an inflation hedge. I've never sold a building, because they generate an income stream that can increase over time, particularly in an inflationary economy. And the buildings themselves keep increasing in value if they are well-built and maintained. These certainly are. That philosophy has served me well over the years. We should hold on to these buildings."

I felt the bottom dropping out of a lucrative deal. "That's true," I countered, "but this is a huge profit, and we can reinvest the funds and replicate the program."

His tone grew resolute. "It's not a good idea to sell these buildings, Harvin. They will be a good long-term investment, more valuable as time goes by."

His answer was NO, and it wouldn't change. Yet I knew we were passing up a phenomenal opportunity. To the surprise of Travelers, we passed on its offer. I consoled myself that but for Ben's investment, we couldn't have built the buildings. He had put up the equity and taken the risk. It didn't matter that his cash equity of less than $200,000 would have reaped an incredible return. That was his call, but intuitively I knew the decision not to sell was a big mistake.

Meanwhile, all of our business segments were flourishing. We owned one of Houston's ten largest homebuilding companies, our land-development company had subdivisions throughout the area, our office buildings were fully leased (with another building under construction), and our title agency and property-management operation were both profitable. We had built a large, successful, respected, multidimensional real-estate company in a very competitive market.

As our projects increased, it became more difficult to inspect them because of the distances and time spent in traffic. Tyler, a licensed pilot for years, began lessons to become a helicopter pilot. After he obtained his license, we bought a half interest in a small helicopter. Though Tyler was an excellent pilot, we never flew together.

One afternoon more than a year after we purchased the helicopter, a Bell Jet Ranger helicopter landed at our office. Tyler announced that it was time we upgraded because ours was too small and slow. He had scheduled a demonstration flight. I couldn't believe what I was hearing! We could not afford a half-million-dollar helicopter and the pilot it would require. I waved the invitation off and left shaking my head.

Finding and evaluating new projects was an ongoing activity for all of our companies, and Tyler and I were actively involved in the process. At times we disagreed about a project, but we usually found a way to reach mutual agreement.

Not long after the Bell helicopter incident, Tyler brought in an earnest-money contract to purchase a small tract of land far west of town. The owner was selling the land and a small, private airport he was operating there. The tract was years away from being developed as a subdivision. Tyler's position was that profit from the airport facility would allow us to warehouse the land until it was ripe for development. Warehousing land for an eventual purpose using a temporary land use to pay for it can be a valid strategy. In fact, we owned a property on I-10 near Gessner that was rented to a golf driving-range operation that carried the land while we worked on the tract's retail development. But with this property, Tyler wanted to manage the airport himself, with our people.

As I saw it, that was too much of a reach. We knew nothing about operating an airport—a complex, high-risk business. Considering Tyler's unbridled enthusiasm for this project, I felt these diverging interests would grow as we became more successful.

I decided to pull the trigger on our buy-sell agreement and offer to buy Tyler out.

Needing financing to make the offer, I called Ernie Deal, president of Fannin Bank, to ask for a loan that would serve as my cash offer to Tyler for his half interest in VDI. After agreeing on most of the details, Ernie, Robert L. Clarke (from Bracewell & Patterson, which represented the bank) and I had lunch to discuss the loan.

As we were eating, Ernie said, "There is one more thing we will need before we commit to make the loan."

"I thought there might be something else, but I've enjoyed the lunch so far," I said with a smile.

He grinned. "I want you to give the bank a second lien on your home and a first lien on the additional lot. I know your aunt holds the first lien on both, but you have a large equity in the property, and I'll bet if you ask her, she'll subordinate her first lien on the lot to us and agree to our taking a second lien on your home."

Surprised by the request, I responded, "She might. But this is our homestead, you know."

"I know that very well, and Bob and I have talked about its enforceability, which is questionable. But, if you'll agree to it, it'll mean that you are absolutely committed to making this acquisition succeed. And by Nancy having to agree also, I, and the bank, will feel comfortable that both of you will make your deal work. Along with the other collateral, we'll be secured as well as we possibly could be."

"That's about as secure as I can make any lender," I replied, and then paused before my cautious response. "But if you insist...I believe I can do that."

I went immediately after lunch to my aunt's apartment to discuss the transaction with her. She consented, and then I drove home to discuss it with Nancy.

Nancy had supported my decision to buy out Tyler, but she was fearful about the amount of debt I would incur to do so. To reassure her, I told her that the profit from just one of our projects would pay off the loan within three years. She seemed to relax a little. Then I broached the bank's final requirement: a lien on our home and lot. I reassured her that

Fannin would not get her signature on any note or guaranty, and that it would not put any of her separate property in jeopardy. But without her agreeing to Fannin's requirement, I could not offer to buy out Tyler. Though apprehensive, she agreed.

In May 1982, I made the offer to Tyler. Under the terms of our buy-sell agreement, he had 90 days to decide whether to sell or buy on the exact terms I had offered. It was a difficult summer. We continued to operate the business as before, yet we knew that by September only one of us would own the company.

Tyler worked diligently to make the purchase himself. I accepted the fact that if he did, I would have more cash than ever before. However, for Tyler to match my offer, he would have to relieve me from most of the liabilities I had incurred at VDI. (This possibility pleased Nancy.) While Tyler had started the business, I felt that I had enabled it to survive and then formed the vision of what the company had become.

Finally, as the ninetieth day approached, Tyler agreed to sell. He left in late August with $3 million in cash, and I emerged with 100% ownership of this vertically integrated company with a new parent, The Harvin C. Moore Corporation (HCMC).

Three

A New Partner

Expanding Arbor Home Corp. was my first order of business. We bought lots in six subdivisions in the Dallas-Ft. Worth area and began building houses. Shortly thereafter, we bought Austin's third-largest homebuilder, which established Arbor in both Austin and San Antonio. In addition, we acquired its mortgage company, an early participant in the new field of securitizing mortgages for sale as bonds (later to become familiar to the public as "mortgage-backed securities").

By the end of 1983, Arbor had become one of the largest single-family homebuilders in Texas.

Around this time at a bar association function, I visited with Bobby McGinnis, Nancy's godfather and senior partner at the old Powell law firm in Austin. "Ben Jr. (Nancy's father) tells me that you're doing very well," he said.

I was thrilled. This was the first compliment I remember my father-in-law paying me. I had been waiting a long time to hear it, even if indirectly. He rarely gave compliments. I swelled with pride. He's noticing.

The real-estate business was benefiting from a number of new statutes and regulations. In the late 1970s, S&Ls were freed from restrictions on the interest rates they paid their depositors and thus could pay rates competitive with banks. Next, the federal deposit insurance agencies (FDIC and FSLIC) raised the amount insured on individual accounts from $40,000 to $100,000. These two events created significant liquidity in banks and S&Ls which stimulated an increase in real-estate lending.

In 1981, the "Reagan tax cuts" increased the depreciation expense allowed on improved property, generally around 35 years down to 15 years. This accelerated depreciation allowed many economically successful projects to report a "loss" for income-tax purposes, which the property owners could claim on their personal tax returns. That produced a surge of investment money into real estate across the United States as Americans invested in limited partnerships to build and own income properties.

Another factor fueling the boom in the real-estate industry was passage of the "Garn-St. Germain Act," which allowed S&Ls to own homebuilding and real-estate development companies. The act was so broadly worded, however, that most any investment seemed permissible.

Spurred by an escalation of the cost of energy, inflation took hold in the economy. In an effort to stem inflation, by 1983 the Federal Reserve Bank had raised interest rates to around 20%, an all-time high.

Meanwhile, homebuilders in Houston were having record years constructing and selling about 30,000 single-family detached units each year. The collective wisdom was that although the energy business was slowing, it would pick up again soon.

As my company grew, I needed access to additional capital. My initial goal was to take Arbor public and, with an infusion of capital, eliminate my personal guarantees of tens of millions of dollars of construction loans. I explored this possibility with several investment banks.

On Valentine's Day, 1984, I got an unexpected phone call from Buddy Lander. After taking early retirement from River Oaks Bank, he was looking for something to do and decided that owning an S&L offered intriguing possibilities.

He suggested we meet that afternoon at River Oaks Country Club, where he told me he had evaluated more than thirty S&Ls and found one that was very "clean." Hardin Savings Association (Hardin) in Silsbee, Texas, was small but could be moved to Houston and grown significantly.

"Why don't we go together and buy it?" he asked.

I was surprised and flattered by his question. It also occurred to me that this might provide another way to acquire much-needed capital. The possibility intrigued me.

Hardin's financial statements did, however, reflect a problem: its portfolio of 30-year mortgages at fixed interest rates were below the rates it paid its depositors. With that negative spread, the S&L could eventually become insolvent.

We knew we could securitize the mortgage portfolio and sell it in the bond market; that's what my mortgage company in Austin did. But there was another hurdle. Under Generally Accepted Accounting Principles (GAAP), when a company sells an asset, it has to recognize the gain or loss. Hardin's mortgage assets were current but earned, on average, about 6% annually. To sell that mortgage portfolio, Hardin would have to discount the value of the portfolio, thereby increasing the yield on those mortgages to a market rate that would entice an investor to buy the bonds. Thus, a loss would be incurred—one large enough to make the institution insolvent.

Hardin was not alone in this dilemma. S&L regulators, recognizing an industry-wide problem yet understanding the need to allow the institutions to sell those mortgages and avoid becoming insolvent, had a solution. S&Ls were allowed to amortize the loss over 40 years, thereby recognizing only 2.5% of the loss each year. With the stroke of a regulator's pen, under what are called "Regulatory Accepted Accounting Principles" (RAAP), the entire S&L industry was saved from insolvency.

Buddy and I asked the Federal Home Loan Bank Board (FHLB) to approve us to purchase Hardin. The process required an independent appraisal of the assets and liabilities of HCMC. When filed, it reflected a market value of $250 million and liabilities of $200 million, virtually every dollar of which I had personally guaranteed.

The FHLB approved our application. Commonwealth Savings Association (CSA) in Houston provided the financing. We closed the loan and bought Hardin in January 1985, pledging our stock in the S&L. I also pledged some HCMC assets and three personal assets worth about $2 million. Buddy said he had nothing to pledge except his Hardin stock.

However, he had the contract to buy Hardin, knew how to manage an S&L, had a large reservoir of banking customers, and, through his relationships, had provided HCMC with several large bank loans during 1984—guaranteeing, with me, their repayment. As the financing was coming together in December, he said he realized that since I was putting up all the additional collateral, I could also set the stock-ownership split.

My answer was that we should own Hardin 50-50, but with a buy-sell agreement similar to the one I'd had with

Tyler. Buddy and I each signed a $4 million promissory note to CSA, both of which were cross-defaulted and cross-collateralized. We were now entwined, the legal and business version of Siamese twins.

At our first Hardin Board of Directors meeting, Buddy was elected chairman, and I was elected vice chairman. His top billing was my idea since Buddy was well known in banking and S&L circles, as well as among the all-important regulatory agencies.

The first real-estate loan Hardin made was a unilateral decision. One afternoon in March 1985, Buddy walked into my office.

"You'll like the loan I just made."

"What?" I was taken aback.

"I've made a loan to Howard Barksdale to build a custom home on Woodway."

"Wait a minute," I blurted, "a loan to Barksdale on a 'spec' house?"

"Yeah, it'll be a good loan and besides, you owe him a favor for getting the financing for your land at Katy."

"No I don't!" I steamed. "I don't owe him anything. I paid him two points as the mortgage broker for that loan. And I thought that was overpaying him. I owe him zip!"

He was unfazed. "Well, this'll be a good lo…"

"Buddy," I cut in, exasperated. "A custom home on Woodway? In this market? How big is the loan?"

"It's $600,000, and it'll be a gorgeo…"

"Buddy!" I interrupted again. "That market is dead, and besides, he's not a custom builder, he's a mortgage broker. He ought to have a qualified buyer for the house on contract before we lend him any money."

He was bent on changing my mind. "I've got the plans in my office. Come take a look. It's on a beautiful lot. He'll have a buyer before long."

I shook him off. "I don't need to see it. I just think that's really risky. No one is selling big custom homes."

Buddy remained in upbeat-salesman mode. "It's slow right now, but by the time he finishes, that market will be back."

"I'd be surprised," I responded glumly.

I didn't like anything about that loan, and I was really steamed that Buddy had acted alone. Tyler had never done that. What had I gotten into? Buddy tried to smooth things over, promising to discuss everything before making a decision from then on. I told him that was the only way our partnership could work.

By our third board meeting, Buddy began leaving the meetings early and turning them over to me. After about half an hour, he grew bored and would head for cocktails at the River Oaks Country Club.

Four

Ominous Events

Nineteen-eighty four was a profitless year for my companies, especially Arbor. Pressure from Wall Street to increase homebuilding sales revenue and market share had led to heavy discounting among Houston's major publicly owned homebuilders. And the oil-and-gas industry had begun to collapse beginning in late 1982. At the end of first-quarter 1985, home sales in Houston plunged. Because Arbor Home Corp. was a "production" (speculative) builder —it would begin building a house without a contract, expecting to sell it during construction or soon thereafter—we watched one statistic obsessively: "Finished Unsold Inventory" (FUI).

On the ninety-first day after completion without a contract, a house becomes a huge problem for the builder: interest costs can no longer be capitalized—they must be expensed each month and hit the bottom line; interest is due in cash every thirty days on a fully funded construction loan; and builder's risk insurance must be maintained.

Arbor had always carried roughly twelve to fifteen houses in FUI in Houston, which was about one house in each of the subdivisions where we built. In one month of 1985, that number jumped to thirty. Within ninety days, we had about 100. Every house we had under construction in Houston was now finished and unsold for ninety-one days or more, representing about $10 million in construction loans in default. We couldn't give a house away. The company had no ability to service that liability. When the problem began to surface, we pulled Arbor out of its six subdivisions in Dallas-Ft. Worth. Next, Arbor Homes of Austin was sold, and I used the profit for working capital—but it was not nearly enough to save Arbor. I shut down the company in the summer of '85.

In October, I called Arbor's 16 lenders together to explain the situation and ask for patience. I assured them that I would not put Arbor in bankruptcy and would honor my guaranty of their loans, provided that we agreed on the amount of the deficiency after the foreclosure of Arbor's houses, and further provided that they gave me enough time to pay them back. Their incentive was that Buddy and I could build Hardin into a valuable institution in time, and my 50% equity would eventually enable me to liquidate the amount I owed them.

Within a week, 15 of the 16 lenders had agreed to accept my personal, unsecured, five-year balloon note for the deficiency on their loans. The one holdout was Ameriway Savings, whose chairman was another Houston developer, Joe Russo.

Ameriway's president, Mike Ballesas, was very upset that I would not pay off Arbor's loan, which was relatively small compared to the other lenders. So, it filed a lawsuit against Arbor and me personally. My plea to all the Arbor lenders had been that if they sued me and received a judgment, I would have to file personal bankruptcy, in which case everyone would have to write off the entire debt I owed them—a deplorable outcome for all involved.

Mike pressed me about why I would not pay Ameriway. I stressed that doing so would constitute a preferential payment, an "act of bankruptcy" that would allow other creditors to put Arbor (and me) in an involuntary bankruptcy proceeding, forcing Ameriway to return the payment to the trustee. It seemed clear to me, but Mike was unmoved and would not withdraw the lawsuit.

A few days later, I met with Dick Collier, chairman of University Savings Association, at the time the biggest S&L in Houston and our single largest lender, with over $40 million dollars in construction loans to Arbor.

"How are you coming with the approvals from your Arbor lenders?" he asked.

"I have 15 of the 16."

His eyebrows went up. "Who's missing?"

"Ameriway, and I'm not optimistic. I owe them less than one percent of what I owe you, and I guess they think that if they keep pressuring, they'll get paid to go away."

His curiosity morphed into anger. "Let me tell you something, and you can tell them this: If you pay them anything, I'll throw your ass into bankruptcy so fast it'll make their head swim." He was defiant.

"I've told them any payment to them would be preferential and wouldn't stand up to a challenge by another creditor," I said, "but it didn't make any difference."

"You tell him to call me," he retorted. "Our only hope is for you to make a go of your S&L, and I'm not letting any two-bit lender prevent that."

I smiled. "I appreciate that, Dick."

But he wasn't finished. Ameriway's demands had unleashed a Texas tempest. "It's bullshit! This isn't the time for barnyard bullying. None of us will collect a dime if you have to take bankruptcy now. And let me tell you something else: I'm not going to come after you personally. We've made a lot of money off of you over the years, and you've handled everything as well as anybody. You don't have to worry about where we stand. You just go concentrate on your business—and tell Ameriway to call me."

I left my meeting with Dick reassured by his confidence. When your biggest creditor agrees with what you're doing, it carries a lot of weight.

Unfortunately, it was immaterial to Ameriway, and it would not back off. In January 1986 it obtained a judgment against me that would become final in 30 days. I walked down the hall to inform Buddy. In a flash, his steel-blue eyes turned ice cold as he called to his secretary, "Get Joe Russo on the line for me."

"Joe," Buddy began the call, "Harvin tells me Ameriway just got a personal judgment against him; and you know what that means—he'll have to file for bankruptcy."

From my side of Buddy's desk, it was apparent that Joe was responding as we had hoped. A meeting was scheduled in a few days to "work with each other."

After that meeting, Ameriway released its judgment against me and accepted my five-year balloon note for the amount of the deficiency on its loan to Arbor. However, there was something of a quid pro quo: To get the release from Ameriway, Joe insisted that Hardin make a loan to one of his companies. We agreed and made the loan.

Not only were homebuilding companies going out of business, office developers were unable to lease their buildings. They became known as "see-through" buildings, since they had no occupants and thus no window shades or blinds to hinder the view from one side to the other. New buildings went un-leased; existing space emptied out. As a result, we lost Corporate Plaza Two by foreclosure and, two years later, Corporate Plaza One as well.

Looking back, it certainly made that earlier decision not to sell the buildings to Travelers all the more painful.

It was a discouraging time—and I took the stress home every night. Harvin was now a senior at Northwestern University, Marian a freshman at Vanderbilt University. There was no one at home but Nancy and me. No one to inject a little diversion into our conversations. No one to smile and talk optimistically about "tomorrow." The loan defaults were becoming my "failures" and mounting as one property after another was given to a lender or put in bankruptcy to give me time to negotiate out of personal liability.

Even our biggest project, Falcon Point, a golf course/country club subdivision in the Katy area, was in Chapter 11 as its lender, First South Savings of Houston, struggled to replace all three of its participating lenders. (They had all become insolvent and could no longer fund their pro rata share of the development loan.) It was a daily struggle to work with these problems while trying to grow Hardin Savings Assn.

Although several lawyer friends had encouraged me to file personal bankruptcy, I simply could not do that. I believed that doing so would destroy the trust my lenders had placed in me. Uncle Charles' advice, driven deeply into my psyche, was compelling me to do everything in my power to avoid personal bankruptcy—the ultimate surrender and disgrace—at all costs.

My future was Hardin. And, maybe, just maybe, the Houston economy would recover soon and bring relief. That had happened a decade earlier. I was ready for an encore. However, the signs were yet to emerge in the energy business, and now, the failure of financial institutions was beginning to dominate the news.

With the real-estate business dead in Houston, and having previously identified Nashville, Tennessee, as a promising housing market within a two-hour, non-stop flight from Houston, we shifted our focus to real-estate development there.

In the fall of '85, Hardin made its first land purchase in Nashville, a 25-acre tract near The Hermitage (Andrew Jackson's home), and developed a 50-lot subdivision called Bret Ridge.

For all of that year, Hardin made a significant profit. We declared a dividend with which we paid the first installment on our loan from CSA. But several weeks after we delivered our checks, CSA's president, Campbell Wood, scheduled an appointment to discuss our payment. Campbell, Buddy and I met in my office.

"We're not going to accept your payment on our note," Campbell said flatly. "The dividend should be retained to augment your capital. We don't want you taking your earnings out in a dividend. You're not strengthening Hardin." He was adamant.

"Campbell," I responded, "we would have preferred not to have paid the dividend, but we had no other way to make our note payment to CSA."

"Well, okay," he replied. "We'll give you a little more time to see if you can't come up with the funds from some other source."

"Campbell, as a practical matter that is the only source we have for the payment. And I don't believe you'll find anywhere in our loan documents that we are prohibited from paying a dividend," I said confidently.

"Unfortunately, you're right," he conceded. "And that is our next point: We are going to revise those loan documents to cover that clearly."

While Buddy listened intently, I argued, "We don't like inserting a restriction like that in the loan documents because no one can predict the future, and we need the flexibility to use the dividend to service our debt."

"Redoing the loan documents is non-negotiable," Campbell asserted.

I knew that if we refused, CSA could "deem itself insecure," accelerate the note and demand full payment, which would force us to either move the loan or pay it off. Both of those courses were impossible. We were not in a strong negotiating position. With just a glance, Buddy and I confirmed our mutual thought.

"Campbell," I injected, "if you will accept that payment, we'll start working with your lawyers to revise the loan documents to your satisfaction."

He nodded. "All right, we'll start on that as soon as we get back to our office."

In early 1986, oil fell below $10 per barrel for the first time since 1973. Analyzing the impact of that sobering news, we believed Hardin was insulated because none of our borrowers were in the energy business, even though housing and real-estate development in Texas would continue to suffer. Therefore, Hardin continued to look for opportunities in Nashville while carefully making new loans in Houston.

As we formulated a revised business plan for Hardin, we considered adding a mortgage company because it could own and service mortgages—collect monthly payments—from throughout the United States, thereby spreading the risk of foreclosure of those mortgages from one state to all 50. And it was a profitable business. I still owned the mortgage firm in Austin that I acquired with the Austin homebuilding company. But it could not do business with Hardin because I owned more than 10% of the S&L. Therefore, I simply gave the mortgage company to Hardin, along with its staff.

By this time, Buddy and I realized that we needed a president to manage Hardin's day-to-day operations. Raymond Oshman, a CPA and chief financial officer at San Jacinto Savings in Houston, was our first and only choice. Raymond understood the arcane world of regulatory accounting and how to organize and manage people in a financial institution. He was studious, a good listener, and worked well with everyone. It took a while, but fortunately, we persuaded him to become our president.

With our growth, we felt that "Hardin" was no longer the best name for our S&L, so we changed it to MeritBanc Savings Association (MSA), included our subsidiary development and mortgage companies under the MSA umbrella, and adopted a common logo. An opportunity to expand the mortgage subsidiary arose unexpectedly when Allied Bancshares had to sell its mortgage company due to a pending merger. With that acquisition, MSA attained a significant presence in the market overnight and began to open loan-production offices and buy mortgage portfolios. We ultimately had offices in nine major cities in four states.

During 1986, our MeritBanc Development Company (MDC) subsidiary acquired another tract near Bret Ridge in Nashville and developed "Southfork". It then purchased a wooded tract along a rocky ridge on the south side of Nashville to develop "Woodlands". It also opened an office for MDC in a building near Nashville International Airport.

With the collapse of Arbor Home Corp. in 1985, and of Village Developers in 1986 (there were no homebuilders to buy its lots), it seemed that my time in Houston was spent mostly dealing with creditors. But with MSA, I believed that my equity would eventually provide the wherewithal to repay what I had guaranteed.

My $3 million loan from Fannin to buy out Tyler had been reduced by more than 85% in the intervening four years, but I could no longer pay it regularly, and the bank was exerting pressure to pay it off or move it. I couldn't do either. My friend Ernie Deal was gone, having moved to Dallas as president of a much larger bank. The banking regulators were demanding that the banks either collect their loans or foreclose and sell the collateral. It was becoming adversarial. In the summer of '86, Fannin finally agreed to renew and extend the loan and told me to come sign it.

When the banker handed me the documents, I realized that Nancy had been added as a co-signer of the note with me. Taken aback, I handed them to the loan officer.

"These documents are wrong. Nancy is not signing anything. I've never agreed to that."

"Well, that's the only way the bank will renew and extend the note," he said with a distinctly defiant tone. "If she doesn't, we'll just foreclose."

Aggravated, I fired back. "Fannin has never asked her to sign anything, it was never a part of the lending agreement, and it's not going to be now. I won't allow her separate property to support this loan. It was never in the deal."

"Harvin, you guys have a lot of equity in that property. We'll never need to go after her separate property. So don't worry about that," he replied.

"Listen, you say that now, but you may not be making the decisions later. No one knows what might happen. She's not signing it—period!"

I was upset and angry. No creditor of mine had a right to get to Nancy's separate property, whatever it was. Besides, I had never mentioned it to any lender, much less offered it. And now, Fannin was trying to slip her into the deal. I was incensed.

As I left, he reiterated that I had to pay the note in full or face foreclosure of the lien on our home unless Nancy signed. My earlier decision to buy Tyler out and obtain the financing had come down to this. It was not something I had anticipated. I was furious at the bank. With no other place to turn, humiliated and desperate, I asked Nancy's father if he could help.

The next morning, at his breakfast table, I explained to Ben the history of the loan and the collateral Fannin held, which would, given time, pay off the loan. Saying only that he would try, he asked me to set up a meeting with the loan officer.

At the meeting, the loan officer laid out the bank's proposal. Ben said nothing as he slowly and carefully looked over the documents. It was one of his negotiating ploys. Finally, he said he would purchase the note and liens from Fannin and, to save paying a legal fee, asked me to draw the papers for him to review. Both the loan officer and I exhaled with relief.

While I had been embarrassed to ask him for help, I was grateful that he had agreed. I knew he would be well secured; I just didn't know how long it would take to pay him back.

Up to that point, I had kept this pressure and stress at the office. But once Ben became involved, I discussed it fully with Nancy. While closing his purchase of the loan was a great relief to me, I don't think it had the same effect on her. She seemed relieved that Fannin was no longer a problem but disappointed that I had sought her father's help. I sensed that it solidified her negative view of me. He had saved our home from foreclosure...but I had failed. Fifteen percent of the loan remained unpaid.

My relief evaporated like morning dew in the sunlight as her reaction sunk in. It made me wonder if I could ever regain her respect or her trust. The irony was that I was steadfastly protecting her separate property while fighting the effects of Houston's awful real-estate market and withering economy. I felt discouraged, unappreciated and alone.

When our next annual payment to Commonwealth was due, we were prohibited from using an MSA dividend to pay it. CSA held as collateral my shares in Capitol Cities Broadcasting Company, which had recently been sold for almost $1.6 million. It applied that amount to both of our loans. Because Buddy and I were cross-defaulted and cross-collateralized under the loan documents, I had no alternative. For the amount that was applied to Buddy's loan, he gave me a promissory note, but I knew in taking it that only from his equity in MSA would I ever be repaid.

CSA still held, as collateral on our loans, two more of my personal assets: an interest in a land partnership worth about $500,000 and Allied Bancshares stock worth about $750,000.

It would take everything in my power to keep those assets. MSA had to survive, and thrive, for me to recoup what I had just lost.

Soon after, MSA's fourth Nashville acquisition renewed my spirit with its vast potential. It acquired two farms, totaling 640 acres, just north of Lebanon Road only two miles from the airport. This land was ideal for a multiuse project and would capitalize on the region's growth spawned by American Airlines' decision to make Nashville a hub, and General Motors' building its Saturn automobile plant in nearby Spring Hill. We named the project "Gateway".

Nashville and Davidson County have a combined government, and its Metro Council implements and enforces its land-use plan and zoning requirements. To develop Gateway, the Nashville Land Plan had to be amended and its zoning reclassified to permit mixed use (i.e., residential, office and retail). The councilman for this area, Sammy Underwood, was in favor of growth and liked our plans for Gateway. The Metro Council operated under a system known as "Councilmatic Courtesy," meaning that if a councilman agreed to a development in his or her district, the entire council invariably would agree. The reverse was also true—a council member's disapproval would almost always result in the council's rejection. We bought Gateway because of Underwood's endorsement of our project.

We began the planning while purchasing additional parcels that would allow us to extend Donelson Road, a major thoroughfare from the airport, north across Lebanon Road and the Stones River to Gateway. It was as exciting and challenging as anything I had ever done.

In the fall of '86, we made a formal presentation to a group of about 20 city leaders in a large conference room in downtown Nashville. There was only one woman present among a sea of dark suits. Except for her black high heels, she fit in wearing a black pin-striped suit and was just as attentive. Concluding our presentation, I spoke for a few minutes summarizing our plans for Gateway.

As I milled around after the meeting near a large drawing of Gateway, the woman approached and introduced herself as Mary Jensen, a commercial photographer who had been asked by one of our consultants to attend and to take pictures for publicity purposes. I couldn't help but notice her brown shoulder-length hair, dark eyes and trim figure. After our brief encounter, she gave me her business card.

Several weeks later I interviewed Mary. I learned that she was divorced, had twin teenage daughters and a son in college at Memphis State (now the University of Memphis). She owned a successful photography business and was on the staff of Nashville Tech, a community college, teaching several photography classes. The following week, we drove all four of our projects to orient her and discuss photography needs. This excursion lasted longer than we had anticipated, so I suggested we eat dinner before parting, and she agreed. Mary was animated about the projects and how they could be presented through her photography. Her enthusiasm was a breath of fresh air.

In Nashville, developers must meet with citizens near their proposed projects and consider their comments before seeking Metro Council approval. We found that sentiment for Gateway was divided. While many in Nashville were "pro growth," not everyone welcomed the "outsiders" that the growth brought nor the developments that they planned.

Mary, it turned out, was more than a photographer. With her background and expertise, she began to put together our presentations to the Metro Planning and Zoning Board, especially for Gateway, often blending into the slide presentations the way we had solved development problems in Houston to illustrate how we might solve similar challenges in Nashville. Over a period of months, we completed the plans for Gateway. By the time of the council election in May 1987, it was ready to be presented for final approval.

Underwood, standing for reelection, was opposed by a "no growth" candidate. All indications were that it would be a very close race. Discussing the race with him, Sammy told us that he would prefer to defer the Gateway Land Plan Amendment and Zoning Change on Metro Council's agenda until after the election.

In a race decided by just a few dozen votes, Underwood lost.

Five

The Choice That Changed My Life

In late 1987, Buddy walked into my office with a despondent look and said he had an income-tax problem. He owed $175,000 and couldn't pay it. I stared at him; his audacity astounded me.

"How could you have a tax liability that big?" I asked.

"It's due to some of my wife's investments."

"Well, then, she should pay it," I asserted.

"That's not possible," he said flatly.

"So, if you don't pay it, the IRS will file a tax lien against you?"

"Right, and that's curtains for both of us. We've got to do something."

"Buddy, your tax problem is not a 'we' problem," I said emphatically.

"Well, if the IRS files that lien, we're in default to Commonwealth on our loan."

He was right. My mind raced through a minefield. Why did he wait until the last minute to solve this? He had to have known about it earlier. Most important, how can I avoid being involved? I was in a sticky situation. We had a buy-sell agreement, but I had no capacity to buy him out. I was stuck.

Suddenly his mood brightened. "We could lend that amount to your cousin, Joe, and then he could funnel it back to us."

I stared at him in disbelief. "Buddy, I can't ask Joe to do that."

"You could if you paid him something for his trouble," he said hopefully.

As I was shaking my head he added, "Let's think about it tonight and talk tomorrow."

Buddy and I met again the next morning. "Isn't there some other way to fund your IRS problem?" I began.

"Can't think of any," he said matter-of-factly.

"What about your cousin Jack Lander. His bank could lend it to you," I suggested.

"Won't work," he quickly responded.

"Buddy, this isn't my problem," I reminded him. "It's your wife's."

"Yeah, but it'll still sink you and me both if they file a tax lien…" His voice trailed off as he fidgeted with his wedding ring.

Quiet settled into the room. I was frantically trying to think of something other than what he had suggested. Finally, Buddy spoke. "The only solution is for us to lend it to Joe. We'll lend him enough to pay him something and give you some funds to service one of your debts. That way we all get some benefit."

"I don't like it," I repeated, shaking my head.

"I don't either, but we have no choice," he said glumly.

The pressure of accommodating his desires and our financial commitments was tremendous, greater than I had ever experienced. But I couldn't just walk away. I couldn't lose MSA. After a few moments, I reluctantly joined Buddy in thinking of reasons why this "solution" would be okay.

MSA was solvent. If Joe later defaulted, the entire loan would simply be charged against MSA's positive net worth; it wouldn't jeopardize MSA's solvency. I also felt, though I did not voice it, that if this became a problem loan I could ask my aunt for help. Buddy and I also took substantial comfort in knowing that all the money we received was paid to the IRS and to another federally insured financial institution. The government was out only what we paid Joe.

Our conversation gravitated toward all the insolvent S&Ls that were flipping properties with fraudulent appraisals to mask their insolvency. That was much worse than this loan. We ended our conversation by simply repeating what we knew deep down: As long as MSA did not go insolvent, no one would ever know about it.

I called Joe and said I wanted to sell him a few assets that I owned, but that MSA would lend him the money to do it. Joe came over that afternoon and agreed to sign a $185,000 loan from MSA, pay Buddy the $175,000 for his income-tax liability, keep one or two thousand dollars, and give me the balance.

I was torn up inside as I talked to Joe. This was not an appropriate way for Buddy to pay the IRS, or for me to service one of my bank loans. On top of that, Joe was agreeing to help us simply because I had asked him and told him that we would find an investment for him that would liquidate the loan in due course. I set up a corporation for Joe and then transferred some leftover assets of marginal value from my personal company to it, thus making the transaction look legitimate and helping me "feel" better. Buddy didn't care how that was done. Having paid the IRS, his discouragement dissipated.

With this loan to Joe, I knew I had crossed the Rubicon and had done so because I did not have the guts to say "No." I was angry at myself, but took some comfort that we had avoided a problem that could have cost us MSA.

After the first of January, 1988, Capital Bank's president called Buddy and demanded immediate payment of our past due, cross-guaranteed notes. Buddy called me in Nashville to give me the news. We had to pay them off, now!

Once again, Buddy was highly agitated and had lapsed into a despondent, debilitating mood. The pressure the bank was putting on him monopolized his attention until it was mitigated. He knew we couldn't pay Capital Bank but was determined that we had to do something.

Among MSA's assets were shares of stock in Capital Bank worth around $600,000 which had secured a defaulted loan. Buddy thought he could use those shares to pay off Capital.

"I'm going to send Joe over to Capital with that stock to pay off our loans."

"No, Buddy!" I almost screamed. "MSA owns that stock. It's not ours."

Immediately, he said with an edge, "That's all we have to get those loans paid."

Trying to calm him, I said slowly, "You just can't take the stock out of our vault and send it over there. Listen, when I get back, I'll go over and tell them we can't pay it."

"No, we can't do that!" he said frantically. "Absolutely not. Without our payment, Capital will be insolvent and we will have caused it. My friends own that bank. I can't let that happen."

"But Buddy, it takes a lot of loan defaults to create insolvency. We're not the only ones responsible for its failure."

"Yes, but if we're the last, we pushed them over the line. I can't live with that. We have to do this. I have the certificates in my hand. I'm sending them over right now."

He was adamant. It was useless to argue with him.

"Well, how are we going to document this?" I inquired, hoping to draw the focus to the ramifications of what he was preparing to do.

"I don't know, but you're smart. You'll figure something out."

I was really worried about this one because Joe, even with my aunt's help, couldn't amortize both of his loans.

We made a loan to Joe for around $600,000, and he paid MSA for the Capital stock. Then he took the certificates to Capital Bank's president, who marked our notes paid. When Joe returned with our notes marked paid, Buddy's mood turned from a dismally dull hue to a bright and sunny color. A problem had been averted. But I was left with the nettlesome problem of how to document it.

While I had strenuously objected, I knew I was just as culpable as Buddy because I ultimately acquiesced, participated and benefited from the arrangement.

By the spring of 1988 we were delinquent in paying Commonwealth on our loan to purchase MSA. We had no way to come up with the $500,000 it demanded. Failure to pay would result in foreclosure on our stock. We would have to file bankruptcy and be forced out of our jobs. Something had to be done immediately. We were lurching from dilemma to deadline to crisis, every day another test. Will it ever end? I wondered.

A longtime friend of Buddy's, a wealthy apartment owner, asked us to finance his purchase of an apartment project from a failed S&L. He needed a $5.3 million loan. Buddy told him we would do it, and I agreed with the terms quoted to him. As the loan closing approached, Buddy said the borrower was going to pay us a $500,000 fee for making the loan but would not be using our loan proceeds to pay us the fee because he had many other sources of funds. Joe's corporation would sell to our borrower an option to buy a tract of land that Buddy and I had obtained for it. The corporation would receive the fee and pay it to us after Joe kept a little for himself. I heaved a big sigh of relief. That would give us the money to pay Commonwealth, but it would not come from the MSA loan. The $5.3 million loan was closed while Nancy and I were in France celebrating our twenty-fifth wedding anniversary.

Some weeks later I learned that our borrower had actually drawn the half million dollars from our loan. I was infuriated. This time wasn't any easier than the first. Each one gnawed on my conscience, and I felt terrible for involving Joe. Yet if Buddy and I made it through this period with MSA, I hoped that nagging fear in my gut would go away.

Six

Deceived and Defeated

During the summer of 1988, with $4 million invested in our Woodlands subdivision and no liens against it, we needed to obtain a $2 million development loan. Being only a few months from completion and having the lots under contract to builders, it would be an attractive loan. At the same time, Joe Russo needed a $2 million loan for an office building he owned, which would be secured with a second lien.

Joe asked us to make that loan and we agreed, provided that Ameriway would simultaneously lend MSA what we needed. All of us breathed a collective sigh of relief.

Ameriway's loan on our Woodlands subdivision was critical because we now could see that MSA might become insolvent later in the year. I was also pursuing a sale of our Gateway project while we sought investors to give MSA a capital infusion.

Our mortgage company was the brightest star among our assets, having grown to a portfolio of about $2 billion with solid, consistent earnings. It alone could carry MSA through a period of losses, if we were permitted to continue to grow it. Therefore, we requested regulatory approval.

Our future and that of our almost 300 employees rested on securing two or more of these alternatives. It was a frantic time, yet a time when my concern, or especially fear, had to be concealed from the employees. I had to be cool, calm and confident at the office—and even more so at home.

In late summer, as I was completing the contract to sell Gateway, the purchaser suddenly announced that it had filed for bankruptcy. What a blow! Down to only three alternatives, we realized that closing the reciprocal loans with Russo and Ameriway was the only one of the three that we controlled, so it became our top priority. During our negotiations, Joe had continually reassured us that Ameriway could, and would, make the loan.

One October morning in Nashville, Buddy called me. "I just talked to our friend, and he says that his lender is going to post his building for foreclosure today if he doesn't bring the mortgage current immediately."

"Well," I said, "then we need to close Ameriway's loan on the Woodlands today, also."

"No—Joe said there's too much to do on our loan to get both closed together."

"Buddy, he's had just as much time as we have. We shouldn't close our loan to him before he closes his loan to us." I was emphatic.

"I know, but he's really in a tight spot," Buddy pleaded.

"Yeah, but look what kind of spot we are in if he doesn't close our loan? We really need that loan on the Woodlands."

"He'll close our loan," Buddy assured. "We need to work with him. And I trust him."

I bore in. "Buddy, he needs to work with us, too. These loans have always been tied together. Ameriway needs to close our loan at the same time, period. Remember, we're getting a second lien and Ameriway's getting a first lien. They're getting the better loan. I really don't like this." Why can't Buddy see this? It's so obvious.

"Well, he's really in a fix and it has to close today. Joe promised me he'd close our loan in the next couple of weeks."

It just didn't feel right. "Buddy, I think we're gambling." I paused before adding, "The problem is, I'm in Nashville covered up with work, and you're there. So, I guess you have to do what you think is best. But I'll tell you again: I do not like not having a simultaneous closing."

"I'll get him to commit to close our loan when you get back," he promised.

Buddy closed Joe's loan that day.

A week had passed when I stuck my head in Buddy's office. "I thought you said he was going to call and give us the closing date."

"He told me that, but he hasn't called. Sit down and I'll call him right now."

From my side of Buddy's desk, I could tell that there was little conversation about our loan, but Joe did agree to an appointment the following week.

Buddy and I drove to Joe's office and waited for him. Finally, he barreled into the conference room and apologized for being late, saying he was under a lot of pressure.

"Well, Joe, everyone in the S&L business is under a lot of pressure," I said with more than a little irritation in my tone. "We won't take but a few minutes of your time. We just need to set the closing on Ameriway's loan on our Woodlands project."

"You'll need to read something first," he said, leaving the room abruptly. He returned in a few minutes, slid a document across the table to Buddy and me, and immediately left to take care of something else. I took one glance and saw the words "Operating Agreement" at the top. Without reading it, I flipped to the last page and noticed that it was dated several months earlier, before we had agreed to these reciprocal loans.

An operating agreement is a document that federal regulatory agencies—such as the Federal Home Loan Bank (FHLB)—use to control what an institution does once the agency assumes it will have to take it over, but before they send in regulators to manage the institution. The agreement severely limits the institution's management authority and the amount of money it can lend. Under this document, Ameriway could not lend more than $250,000.

I looked at Buddy. "We've been screwed."

"I...don't...believe this!" he stammered.

"Well, there it is in black and white. He knew from the beginning that Ameriway couldn't make the loan to us. He's got our money and we're out in the cold."

Buddy looked down silently. Joe walked back into the room.

"You knew this all along!" I said, tossing the document on the table. "You knew you couldn't do your part of our deal."

"Well," he said matter-of-factly, "times are tough all over, and you gotta do what you gotta do."

I narrowed my gaze. "Yeah, I guess so."

We got up and walked out. I was seething. How does someone you think you know stiff you like that? Anger mingled with disbelief. Who can I trust? And, what was Buddy thinking?

As we drove back to the office, I began to calm down. We were in dire straits and desperately needed that Ameriway loan. But I had to shake it off, not dwell on it. Somehow, some way, we had to find another solution.

While I didn't talk in the car, Buddy kept saying, "I can't believe it, but we'll find a way. We'll find a way."

About this same time, our request for regulatory approval to increase our deposits in order to grow our mortgage company was denied. We had few alternatives left.

In the fall, MSA became insolvent and we asked the FHLB—before they removed Buddy and me and took it over—to give us until the end of the year to find an acquirer, or to recapitalize. If unsuccessful, Buddy and I agreed to resign. To appease the FHLB and obtain its agreement, Buddy and I cut our salaries, instead of cutting all executive salaries as it had requested. It wasn't fair to reduce their salaries; we were the owners.

Raymond Oshman, our president, prepared the investment proposal and he, along with Buddy and me, began the search. This task was added to my weekly trips to Nashville to keep those projects moving. At the end of every day I was dead-dog tired.

The pressure was relentless and mounting. If we failed, we would lose MSA and regulators would search every file to discover anything improper. That was scary! They wouldn't like those loans involving Joe Westerlage. A shiver went down my spine. I tried to think about something else—anything else.

Nashville, however, was a safe harbor. With Gateway, we had finally developed a revised land plan that our new councilman could support, though he was not ready to support any zoning change. Our other developments were finished or on schedule and gave us a sense of accomplishment. Although

Mary had not taken photos for us in more than a year, she continued to provide me with citizen reaction to our revised Gateway plans.

While she was becoming a quiet refuge from my swirling storm, I was terribly conflicted as I began to feel an emotional attachment to her. I wanted to run from that, and from her, but I couldn't. It was the only place of solace that I felt I had. It didn't seem important to her that I could end up in bankruptcy and lose everything. "Stuff" just didn't matter to her. She also recognized the deep struggle I was having about seeing her, but she never pushed me in any direction. This was my problem, or mine and Nancy's, to work out, but Mary understood how unhappy both of us were. She did care about me as a person, however, and hoped that there might be a future for us. But whatever happened, she was certain I would recover and be okay.

During December, Buddy and I got an offer from Robert Dedman, chairman of Club Corp of America ("CCA") in Dallas, who, under the regulators' "Southwest Plan", had purchased three S&Ls in Texas, but none in Houston. I told him that Buddy and I would not get a single dollar for our stock, nor an employment or consulting contract. We would simply give him the keys and leave. Considering MSA's $400 million in assets, $325 million in deposits, 285 employees, relatively few bad loans and a thriving mortgage subsidiary, he was an eager acquirer.

On December 18, he informed the regulators of his desire to acquire MSA and asked for an extension until January 31, 1989, to consummate the purchase. But after Christmas, the regulators responded, "No Extension." I was absolutely devastated! The regulators would now take over MSA. My future looked bleak!

That week I moved my personal office furniture from MSA into a small storage unit and went home to face bankruptcy, a disintegrating marriage and no job prospects. On December 30, the regulators took complete control of MeritBanc Savings.

Seven

The Trials

In early January, 1989, I trudged up the echoing metal stairs to the barren, cold room over our garage, dropped a box stuffed with my files on the gray linoleum floor, and turned on the small electric heater next to the metal folding chair and card table.

This was now my office. There was a small bathroom and telephone in the room so I did not annoy Nancy. I was out of sight, but hardly out of mind.

I began to prepare the schedules of my meager assets and almost $70 million of unsecured debt. While my law-school friend, Raymond Kerr, would represent me, I had to locate, assemble and summarize the information for him. It was grim, depressing work as each file represented business associates who had relied on me to pay them.

Often, my work was interrupted by the knock of a deputy sheriff at the door serving notice of another lawsuit against me for many of those debts. With the filing of my bankruptcy, the burden of dealing with those lawsuits would end.

Each week, Nancy and I had appointments with our respective psychological counselors as we struggled with the massive problems we individually faced; then we would meet together with our marriage counselor. For my part, I was trying to fathom the depth and intensity of the trauma I was enduring in business, together with understanding the source and depth of Nancy's fears and how to cope with them. With a relationship that had grown more distant over the years and lacked any deep common bond other than our kids, we had both become almost incapable of understanding the other's position and feelings. At the same time, both of us found the idea of divorce an anathema. We were working hard to find ways to preserve the marriage, despite the trauma and uncertainty of what each new day might bring.

Discussing our future at an early January session with our marriage counselor, Nancy tearfully asked me, "What are you going to do now?"

"Well, I'll just do what I've been doing, develop real estate," I said matter-of-factly.

"You can't do that. You're broke and you can't borrow any money, either."

"I know, but I'll ask some friends to invest in my deals."

"No one is going to do that. Everything you've ever done is a failure."

That statement switched the light on. The root of her fear was of any kind of failure, and I was now the epitome of that. Even as her words stung, through the pain I realized that she could not tolerate failure in her world. And my world certainly involved failure, or high risks that could lead to it.

It was becoming clear: This was a hopeless relationship for both of us. Divorce was certain, the only question was how soon. Nancy and I agreed that when my bankruptcy was completed, we would seek the divorce.

Around the middle of January, I got a call from Mary. She had moved to Houston. I was quite surprised. We had pulled back from each other as I was more and more consumed with my overwhelming problems, and she knew that those had to be resolved whether we ever saw each other again or not.

Mary said she needed to redirect her photography career and wanted a change in location. She felt prospects in Houston might be better as the economy here was beginning to turn, and she had almost moved here five years before.

I really had thought that I might not see her again, so I was excited to hear from her and promised to introduce her to my friends who might help her get established. When she asked how I was coping with all of my problems, I knew she still cared and I wanted to see her.

After all my struggles to avoid bankruptcy, I finally filed it on February 9, 1989. Except for my home, car and a few items of personal property, everything I had acquired over the years was now lost. The unraveling at times had seemed to proceed in slow motion, yet at other times it seemed to move at warp speed. And I didn't have a job, not even the prospect of one. Zero income. Fortunately, Nancy paid all the household expenses.

This had been my third brush with bankruptcy, and this time I couldn't avoid it. I prayed for the courage and strength to deal with what it might bring.

My bankruptcy was classified as a "No Asset" case. At the First Meeting of Creditors, a lawyer representing the Resolution Trust Corporation ("RTC"), which had taken over all of the insolvent S&Ls, zeroed in on one particular transaction at MSA and aggressively questioned me. After an hour or so, the court, noting this was taking much longer than it had expected, adjourned the meeting. I left completely shaken as I realized that the RTC was probably going to challenge everything I had done at MSA. My instinct told me this could get much worse.

Continuing to work from my garage "office," I began to search for a job. After a month or so, John Eikenburg offered a free office if I would solicit legal work for his firm. I leaped at the offer, reclaimed my office furniture from storage, and began officing with Eikenburg & Stiles in the same building where Bracewell & Patterson was when I practiced law. I was back in my comfort zone.

Meanwhile, Mary was also looking for a job. She had underestimated her ability to establish her photography business, and shortly after moving here, some of her photography equipment was stolen. Without enough money to replace it, she needed to change professions.

In July, I learned that my instincts were justified: Raymond told me the RTC was going to file an objection to my discharge in bankruptcy based on fraud and would be especially critical of the loans to Joe Westerlage. I cringed. This was serious and could evolve into a criminal case, too.

Buddy had filed bankruptcy a month after I had, so I asked Raymond if the RTC would do the same thing in Buddy's case. He didn't know, but assumed it would.

Nancy was horrified. As she read the RTC's objection, she broke into tears and asked, "How in the world could you have misapplied $110 million of MeritBanc's assets?"

"Those are the RTC's allegations. I didn't do that, it's not true!" I said loudly.

"Well, you must have or they wouldn't have said it. Oh, this is just too horrible, horrible…"

After a long pause, I took a deep breath. "Nancy," I began, "it's time to file the divorce. I simply can't take having to fight all of these problems every day and then come home with you taking their position. I just can't deal with that."

She didn't respond; she just remained quiet except for her intermittent sobs. It angered me that she had never given me even one word of encouragement. It was very clear to me now where this case was heading, and I would be in a fight for my freedom—a fight against the U.S. government.

With guidance from her father, beginning well before we were married, Nancy had kept meticulous records about her separate property. And it was several years after we were married before Ben had even given her the stock certificates that she owned. By law, however, the dividends from those investments were classified as income to the community, and thus subject to community debts. The claim by the RTC in bankruptcy was a claim only against our community, but, if successful, it could also seize the income from her separate property.

The value of her listed stocks was obvious. We incorporated their dividends into our tax returns each year and paid the taxes from my earnings. But I had never heard the value of her other separate property. In fact, I don't think Nancy knew the full extent of it. Her father had always handled everything.

Still, the mere suggestion that the RTC might be able to claim any of her separate property fed her unfounded belief that she would be left destitute. In addition, she lived with the daily recognition that her father was slowly dying from cancer. It was an agonizing time for her as well.

All the while, I continued to live at home with Nancy's acquiescence as I could not afford even a small apartment.

But driving home each evening seemed partly normal, yet surreal. I felt like a "squatter," although it was my home and had been in my family since 1957. It would be very hard to part with it, but in the fall we decided to sell the house, as Nancy did not want to continue living there. By November, my being in the house made it so uncomfortable for her that she asked me to move out. I consented. My only affordable option was sharing my parents' apartment that they used when they came to Houston. Even though I left my things in the house until it sold, it was gut-wrenching to leave it.

After several months with Eikenberg & Stiles, I suggested I could do more for them if I set up a title-insurance agency. They agreed. By the end of the year, Village Title Company was up and running—and I finally had a modest monthly income.

In December, Nancy called to tell me that the IRS wanted to examine our tax records. From the agitated tone of her voice, I knew she was upset. "Evidently you have another problem, which will probably become my problem too," she said tersely.

"That doesn't indicate a problem," I replied. "They're entitled to look at those records."

"Well, you'd better call them back right away!" she said, as if I might not.

Having always commissioned independent, certified audits of all of my companies by a large, national accounting firm (which also prepared and filed my tax returns), I was happy to comply with no fear of impropriety. About three weeks later, however, I received an IRS letter stating that I owed an additional $1.1 million of income tax. I was flabbergasted—but Nancy was livid.

"How could you?!" There was no acceptable explanation. "The IRS said it, so you must owe it!"

Fortunately, Raymond was also an experienced tax attorney. We responded by filing a lawsuit against the IRS in U.S. Tax Court in Washington. I knew this was going to be expensive, but I didn't owe anything. I had to fight back, but now I began to be a little paranoid. It seemed as if everybody was scrutinizing everything I had ever done, determined to discover wrongdoing. And to Nancy, it was all justified. I had been too much of a wheeler-dealer.

We sold our home in January 1990. The movers headed for Nancy's new home, not far away, with all of her furniture and belongings, including all of our wedding gifts, which are presumed under the law to be gifts to the bride. We divided the more sentimental items.

My parents agreed that I could store my few possessions in Chappell Hill, across the street from their Stagecoach Inn at a house they called Lottie's, which was part of their bed-and-breakfast operation. I hired two young men to help load the boxes of my books, tools, greenhouse plants and a few pieces of furniture into my Suburban and trailer. It was a hard, tiring and lonely task that took much longer than I had anticipated because I did not want to leave anything, not even the broken clay pots in the green house.

As the last bulging boxes were loaded, the men climbed into the Suburban and slowly pulled the trailer down the driveway to the street. Standing in the house's entryway, I pushed the front door shut and turned to face, after 16 years, my empty home.

Each step echoed off the walls as I walked upstairs to make my final check. At the top, I turned left and walked slowly into Marian's blue, but barren, bedroom. The bare oak floor and the empty bookcases—which only a few days before had held her favorite books, dolls, pictures and other mementos—punctuated the stillness. Suddenly, the immensity, the finality of what I was losing overwhelmed me.

I slowly slid to the floor lost in grief and murmuring, "Why me, God, why me?"

After a long silence, my tears had stopped and I heard a distant voice utter a single sentence. I strained to listen. There it was again.

"...because I'm not through with you."

Even though my mother (whom I called "Mimi") consistently suggested "wonderful" women for me to date, she knew I was seeing Mary regularly—and didn't like it. It escaped her that Mary provided a stabilizing influence as my legal battles increased. With every added burden, Mary expressed confidence in a positive outcome and that I could handle whatever happened. In fact, the worse it got, the stronger she became. With each passing day, I realized how much her presence helped and strengthened me. I loved and needed her. Mary's managerial job at a video-dating service for young professionals meant working afternoons and evenings, but we often saw each other after she got off work.

The RTC lawyers advised Raymond they would take only one more deposition—mine, and it would be videotaped.

"Weren't they going to depose Buddy, too?" I asked Raymond. He didn't think they would. And in fact, they never took any depositions in his bankruptcy case. He knew as much as I did, more in some instances. Why was I their sole target of interest? It was grossly unfair that I had to bear all the expenses, time and energy of discovery.

Soon after the RTC filed the fraud action, Raymond suggested I retain defense attorney Bill Burge, even though there was no criminal proceeding. I did so immediately.

Just before my deposition, I met with Raymond and Bill, who insisted that I not answer any questions except who I was and where I lived. Thereafter, I was to "take the Fifth Amendment" on the grounds that my answer might incriminate me. I didn't want to do this, but Bill was insistent. The day-and-a-half deposition was grueling and left me mentally and physically exhausted.

Shortly after that, Bill called to say that he had heard a federal grand jury was looking at something involving MSA. He suggested that together we call the U.S. Attorney's office for an appointment. On the call, the prosecutor responded, "There's no need for that. The grand jury indicted your client this morning."

Bill stammered in disbelief. "You've...already indicted him?"

"Yes, along with Buddy Lander and Joe Westerlage."

I stared at Bill hanging up the phone. "I've been indicted? For what?" I asked incredulously. My mind immediately went into overdrive. Why didn't I get a "target" letter? Bill didn't know. I had no time to adjust psychologically. What was next?

Then it hit me. Publicity is next. This will be in the newspapers, on radio, maybe even TV. I'll be painted as a criminal. Public scorn will follow. How can I survive the humiliation?

Clearly, I had to let my family and friends know about the indictment before they heard or read about it. That afternoon and evening, I made those painful calls. Without a doubt, the two most difficult were to my son Harvin, a national bank examiner in New York City, and my daughter Marian, who was working in Dallas. Later that evening I called John Eikenberg at the title company, and my new consulting client, L.D. Blackwell who owned Blackwell Plastics. They were supportive and assured me that I was to keep working just as I had been. I let out a huge sigh of relief. I needed those jobs and that income, particularly since I was moving into my own apartment in a few weeks.

My father had enjoyed a successful and prominent career as an architect in Houston—designing, for example, the chapel and student center on the Rice University campus, the federal office building in downtown Houston, and, with three other firms, the Johnson Space Center for NASA in Clear Lake, a Houston suburb. In 1980, he had retired to Chappell Hill, northwest of Houston, and turned his firm over to my younger brother, Barry. Now in his mid 80s, my dad's health was declining.

After the indictment, my parents urged me to spend the following weekend with them. As I walked into their home I broke down and sobbed.

"I'm so sorry."

Mimi put her arms around me and just held me. Then she released me and stepped back, becoming her old fighting, defiant self.

"I know you did nothing wrong. We just have to fight this indictment. How much money do you need?" she asked.

I shook my head. "I can handle it. I don't need anything," I answered, trying to sound brave.

"Well, whatever you need, you know we'll do it. Anything."

Daddy, from his wheelchair, observed my grief and simply said, "Son, we'll help you any way we can."

Over that weekend, I built a deck at Lottie's—a needed amenity and a form of therapy that only wielding a hammer and striking a nail can provide. I felt comfortable surrounded by my potted plants, tools and even the old John Deere garden mower I had used to cut the grass at Wimberley.

On Sunday evening, I stood near the back door of the Stagecoach Inn saying goodbye, cradling the baked chicken and blackberry cobbler Mimi had prepared for me. As I moved to leave, Daddy grabbed my arm, pointed his index finger at me and said firmly, "Harv, there are one billion Chinese that have never heard of Harvin Moore!"

Pausing to let the words sink in, he continued, "So you just go about your work and don't wallow in self-pity. Everyone has problems, and their own problems are more important than yours. In three days, they'll forget what yours are. Keep your chin up."

I laughed at my dad's effort to get me to lighten up. And I knew he was right.

A few days after the indictment, Bill and I appeared before a federal magistrate and I entered a "not guilty" plea in the matter of "The United States of America vs. Harvin Cooper Moore, III, aka Harvin Cooper Moore, Jr." I was immediately released on a $500,000 personal-recognizance bond, which requires no cash deposit, but if I failed to appear in court I would personally owe the full amount.

Through the summer and fall of 1990, all the cases were active. Unlike my tax case, the government had the burden of proof in the criminal case. I was innocent until proven guilty, and I had very rational reasons for what I had done.

From the beginning of the criminal case, I had told Bill that I always wanted him to level with me. No sugar-coating.

I would have to deal with whatever materialized, so give it to me straight. Bill and I went over our defenses and analyzed what the prosecutors were relying on in their case. If I went to trial and lost, mandatory-sentencing guidelines would dictate four to five years—in prison. I tried to put that out of my mind.

At one point, the prosecutor called Bill to inquire when I was going to plead guilty. Bill squashed that idea but told me the ploy was typical in criminal cases, and was usually coupled with an intimation that additional charges might be added to the indictment. I realized that the power of the federal government is immense, but I would fight it. They would not steamroll me.

Later, Bill relayed to me a totally different message from the prosecutor. "He said if you can give them, and I quote, 'two scalps,' then you'd probably get probation."

"Bill," I replied slowly, "I can't give them two scalps. I know who they're after in the S&Ls, but we didn't do business with them, nor did I in my company."

"Well, that's what he said, so just file it in the back of your mind."

This was discouraging. First the feds threaten, then they tempt. There was no way I could provide them with the information they wanted. Yet as a lawyer, I knew even slam-dunk cases often turn out the other way in the unpredictable hands of a jury. Probation was clearly a tempting offer.

Simultaneously, negotiations continued between Raymond and the RTC in my bankruptcy case to determine what it would take to settle its objection to my discharge. Finally all agreed that if I could pay one-half million in cash by February 25, 1992, the RTC would release its objection. Otherwise,

I would owe $1.25 million, close to the total of the transactions we did with Joe Westerlage. Using my share of the proceeds from the sale of my home, I made an initial payment of $100,000 toward the $500,000. I was seeing some investment opportunities at Village Title; perhaps one or two would materialize and allow me to meet the deadline.

I sure hoped so.

Eight

Guilty

A s I replayed those three transactions in my mind, I still felt a nagging uneasiness about them. But I kept telling myself that every dollar I received, I paid to another federally insured institution. No one, not even the government, lost a single dime.

Meanwhile, the tenor of the times did not help my cause. Newscasts were regularly reporting S&L and bank failures and citing fraud as the reason. Bumper stickers appeared proclaiming, "Jail the S&L Crooks." I didn't think I was one of them, but the government evidently did.

Drawing down most of my IRA, I was able to pay Bill's retainer. I knew, however, that if I had a lengthy and complex trial, as mine would surely be, I would owe additional legal fees. Where would I get that money? I tried not to think about that either.

Part of trial preparation involved reading and understanding the case law that interpreted the statutes under which I was indicted. As I plowed through them, it became clear that what I had done with the money was not the crime, nor was it a viable defense. The fact that I hadn't squandered it might lessen the punishment, but nothing more. I felt my stomach knot and my throat tighten.

My defense, then, would rest on the fact that MSA was solvent when we did those transactions, and I took the risk since my equity would be eroded if we lost any money. But case law didn't support that theory either. The solvency of the institution was irrelevant. The critical issue was whether the loan was legitimate or just a mechanism to get the funds to Buddy and me. To support my not-guilty plea, I would have to testify, looking twelve jurors in the eye and telling them I did not intend to take any MSA money.

But deep down, I knew I had intended to get the money. That's what had always made me feel so uneasy. Buddy and I had intended to get the money because we had no other way to service our debts and avoid bankruptcy. My uncle's words still resonated in my mind. I couldn't go bankrupt, no matter what.

Probing my conscience and memory, I began to retrace my steps and realized that what I had done was succumb to pressure—albeit intense pressure—to service my debts and thereby avoid taking personal bankruptcy, which also would have cost me my job. I had rationalized my decision. But it was wrong. I was guilty, and I couldn't hide behind those rationalizations any longer. It was time to admit it and pay the price.

When I told Mary what I'd decided to do, she put her arms around me, kissed me, and said that she loved me and would stand by me no matter what.

In late February, Bill and I appeared before David Hittner, a federal judge in the Southern District of Texas, and I entered my plea.

"Guilty."

As I left the courthouse that day, a tremendous burden lifted from my shoulders. I had told the world, "Yes, I did do those things, and they were wrong. I am very sorry and I will accept my punishment."

In the Houston newspaper the next morning, February 22, 1991, on the front page of the Business section, it was reported that Harvin Moore had pled guilty to bank fraud at MeritBanc Savings Association "...and would be sentenced in a building his father designed."

I was disgusted, embarrassed and sad for my Dad, who had nothing to do with what I had done. The reporter was just looking for an "angle" to make his article a little more sensational by adding my father's name.

I can only appreciate vicariously the pain and humiliation that my family felt. And though I can apologize and accept punishment for what I did, I cannot undo it—ever. It's like dropping a pebble into a pond. As soon as it hits the surface, ripples extend outward. We don't know where they will go or what they will cause, just that they keep going.

Three days later, Buddy entered his own guilty plea.

Then began the next phase of my case: meeting with the prosecutors to discuss other MSA loans. On several occasions, I was asked to explain complicated real-estate transactions to the government's inexperienced lawyers and investigators. In those cases, I never knew the institutions or parties involved; that information was always deleted from the documents.

After every conviction, the U.S. Probation Department prepares the pre-sentence investigation (PSI) report, an extensive document containing personal, medical, psychological and criminal histories about the defendant, along with information about the criminal case itself. The PSI becomes part of the defendant's permanent record. It is reviewed by the judge before sentencing, used by the Federal Bureau of Prisons

(BOP) to determine where to incarcerate the defendant and under what special conditions (if any), and referred to by the prison staff in administering its rules and regulations. (For example, if a prisoner's PSI noted his offense had involved a gun, he would not be allowed to leave the 25-acre camp and work on Fort Bliss as other inmates might.) In my case, it turned out to be a much more important document than anyone first thought.

An initial sentencing date was set, but the prosecutors extended it several times so that I could continue to be available to meet with them. Bill said the more information I could provide, the more likely they would recommend "downward departure" from the sentencing guidelines. He continued to believe they might recommend probation.

It soon became apparent that while Buddy and I had both pleaded guilty, I was the only one the prosecutors called to assist them. I really couldn't understand that, but I hoped they'd recognize the extent of my cooperation and would recommend a more lenient sentence.

About this time, Bill called with good news: Joe had pleaded guilty and, instead of going to prison, he'd be fined $25,000 and put on probation for five years. I was relieved.

On many weekends, Mary and I would drive up and down Galveston Bay looking at houses. Mary was drawn to the water, having been raised in West Allis, a suburb of Milwaukee near Lake Michigan. I had loved Wimberley and its Cypress Creek. We both wanted to live on the water, if possible, but still close to Houston.

We made several offers on Galveston Bay houses, but nothing materialized. Our favorite house, in spite of its redwood siding painted pink, was southeast of Houston in Seabrook on Todville Road. This weekend house was too expensive for us. Then out of the blue, the seller's realtor said that the owner had significantly reduced the price. After acknowledging that the new price was reasonable, I told the realtor we could only buy it if the owner would carry a 30-year mortgage. The owner agreed.

Mary and I were ecstatic. At that time, the house was under lease to four foreign astronauts working with NASA at the nearby Johnson Space Center in Clear Lake. Their lease payments equaled the monthly mortgage payment. I had just enough money to make the down payment. I also disclosed my status as a convicted felon awaiting sentencing to the seller, who said it didn't matter as long as we felt we could make the mortgage payments.

Around Labor Day, Mary and I flew to Milwaukee to celebrate her parents' fifty-eighth wedding anniversary and visit her other relatives in the area. Although we enjoyed everything about the trip, I was constantly aware that one day soon I would be sentenced. Her family dealt with it as something I had to "take care of," and then everything would return to normal. To be accepted wholeheartedly and nonjudgmentally by Mary's family was very gratifying to me.

Toward the end of that trip, I got a call from Bill saying that the sentencing had been postponed again until October 21. Another month of waiting. Upon Bill's recommendation, I asked four close friends to write a letter of recommendation to the judge asking for leniency. Those letters were submitted before my sentencing.

As Monday, October 21, 1991, approached, I held out hope that another extension might be given, as prosecutors were still working on several matters. During the summer, I had testified twice before federal grand juries about two separate loan transactions at MSA, both involving the controlling stockholder of other S&Ls. The longer I was available and cooperating with them, the better chance I felt I had that they would recommend probation.

The morning finally arrived. I put on my navy blue suit with a matching tie, drove with Mary to the federal courthouse, and took the elevator with Bill to Judge Hittner's courtroom.

Mary reluctantly sat down on the first row as I walked through the gate and took a seat at the defense table. Looking around the courtroom, I felt a deep sadness, knowing that after today I would no longer be an attorney.

Bill, who had gone to talk with the prosecutors, returned and said he had been told they were in Judge Hittner's chambers. Startled, I asked, "How can that be? I thought both sides were supposed to be present if there was a meeting in chambers."

"Well," he shrugged, "that's the way it is here. They're probably reviewing your PSI." We had been given the completed PSI only a few days earlier.

"But there's stuff in there that isn't correct!" I blurted. "We haven't been given a chance to question it or point out where it's wrong. Until then, they shouldn't be reviewing it with the judge!"

Bill noted that the prosecutors had told him the PSI would not be very important since I had pleaded guilty and cooperated with them.

At that moment, the prosecutors returned to the courtroom and Bill walked over to talk with them. I watched intently as their conversation grew more animated. Bill was obviously arguing with them. Shortly, the prosecutors left the courtroom and Bill came back to the table. I looked up at him with a frown.

"They are not going to recommend probation," he said.

"What?!" I almost shouted. He repeated his words, and my heart sank.

"I've done everything they asked of me." Bill nodded. I had even helped their new staff members understand real-estate transactions and the financing alternatives used. What more could I have done? I looked at the floor and grimaced.

I felt a hand on my shoulder. It was Raymond Kerr, who had come down to support me.

Suddenly the judge entered the courtroom, and all rose silently. The clerk called the first case: "The United States of America vs. Harvin Cooper Moore, III".

With my stomach doing cartwheels and my mouth as dry as cotton, I stepped to the bench, Bill on my left and the prosecutors on my right. With a stern look, the judge asked the prosecutors if they had a recommendation.

"No recommendation, Your Honor."

I couldn't believe what I was hearing. Out of the corner of my eye, I could see Bill's shoulders sag. They weren't even recommending downward departure? Is Judge Hittner going to follow the guidelines after all? Just as that fear gripped me, Judge Hittner asked if I wanted to say anything.

Choking up, in a few words, I reaffirmed that I had broken the law, apologized for what I had done and asked forgiveness for the pain it had caused my family and friends.

I kept my eyes on the judge as he solemnly intoned, "I sentence you to two years in prison, three years of supervised release and $573,925.83 of restitution."

Shock washed over me. I felt as if my knees would buckle and I would collapse to the floor. I steadied myself and fought back tears—tears of disappointment, of anger and of fear. I felt betrayed. This was final, there was no appeal. I was going to prison for two years.

My next recollection was of standing in the hallway outside the courtroom as Mary, my family and several friends hugged me and offered their support and condolences.

Just then, Raymond stormed angrily out of the courtroom holding a piece of paper. He said, "As I stood to leave, an RTC representative gave me this list of things they have asked the IRS to investigate, because the RTC thought you might have gotten money from these and not paid income tax on the funds."

I already faced one tax case. Now I was going to have to fight another one, all because of the RTC's suspicions? I was livid. What's fair about any of this? I wondered. Are these government agencies trying to destroy me and leave me penniless? It felt like the RTC had ripped its pound of flesh from me and was now tossing me to the IRS saying, "Here he is; it's your turn." When would this sordid mess end?

I did, however, control my emotions enough to ask Raymond what would happen to my tax and bankruptcy cases while I was gone. His answer was simple: "Nothing. They will be put on a shelf to await your return, and I'll monitor them to make sure nothing happens that will be prejudicial to you."

As my friends and family began to leave, Bill told me to go to the Probation Office, then to the U.S. Marshal's office to begin initial processing into the prison system. After that, I could go home and wait. In about three weeks, I would get a letter from the Bureau of Prisons advising me to which prison I was to report and when.

As I waited in the Probation Office, Buddy walked in. "You sure dropped me in the grease," he growled. "You should have told me you were going to plead guilty."

Surprised, I said, "Buddy, like you, I hired the best lawyer I could, and his advice was that I could not talk to you, or anyone else, about this case, period."

As I finished the sentence, my probation officer called me back to his office.

When I had completed my probation session and the U.S. Marshals had photographed and fingerprinted me again, I returned to the hall outside Judge Hittner's courtroom where Mary waited anxiously. I now knew that I would not only lose my law license, but also my life, property and casualty insurance licenses. Further, I would not be permitted to vote until five years after I returned from prison and could never own or possess a firearm without a federal permit.

I was thankful that Mary was waiting for me despite these crushing setbacks. We drove home in silence as we tried to comprehend what had happened.

That evening, my Dad, who had been unable to attend the sentencing, called to commiserate with me. As usual, he lifted my spirits by ending the conversation with a light touch: "It won't all be bad; maybe you'll get to meet Mike Milken or Pete Rose."

Several days later, Mary and I met the seller of the house on Todville Road. I explained my sentence but said that we still wanted to buy the house. However, we would understand if he wanted to tear up the contract and return our earnest money.

He didn't hesitate. "Harvin, I know how much you all want this house. As long as you are comfortable that you can make the payments, I'll sell it to you."

With that settled, Mary and I excitedly moved forward with the closing.

On November 8, I received a letter from the BOP assigning my prison number and telling me to report by 2 p.m. on December 16 to the Federal Prison Camp on the Fort Bliss Army base in El Paso. I asked Bill to ask the prosecutors if I could surrender after Christmas instead; they and the court concurred, so the BOP reset the date for January 3, 1992.

Mary and I drove to Milwaukee for Thanksgiving and to celebrate Christmas, too, with her mother and father. At our last dinner together, Mary's mother Irene, a petite, ever-smiling lady, said she knew I'd get along fine.

"As soon as you get back, we'll all go out to dinner and celebrate," she smiled.

All Weston and Irene Jensen really knew was that Mary was in love with me, and I with her. That was all they needed to know. I had become a part of their family and they would love me unequivocally—all the more astounding when I considered what my mother's reaction might be if the shoe were on the other foot!

As we packed to come home early Saturday morning, Mary was searching for something. I handed her a small box and said, "Is this what you're looking for?" She took it quizzically and looked inside.

Her eyes fixed on an engagement ring.

She gasped, and tears of joy filled her eyes. "I would love to be your wife."

We would get married as soon as I returned from El Paso. Excitedly, Mary ran to the kitchen to tell her parents. They were overjoyed. After hugs and a sad goodbye, Mary and I left for the long drive back to Houston. Little did I know it was the last time I would see Mary's mother.

The Moore family's Christmas Eve celebration was at my son Harvin's new home in Houston. He had completed his service commitment to the Comptroller of the Currency as a National Bank Examiner, earned his MBA from New York University, and returned to Houston to take a job. Christmas Eve was always special, but this one was filled with apprehension as we all knew it would be our last one together for some time.

Preparing to report to prison, I had many business loose ends to tie up. While L. D. Blackwell had to find someone else to handle his real estate, I could consult with Village Title Company while I was in El Paso. Village agreed to continue paying me a monthly consulting fee, a huge help to Mary while I was gone.

Raymond, too, had been working with me to get my legal matters put on hold. When I returned, the IRS would resume arguing that I owed them $1.1 million. The RTC was waiting to see whether the $400,000 would be paid; if not, I would owe it $1.15 million. On top of that, I owed restitution of $573,925.83 to the federal court. Finally, after almost 30 years as a lawyer, knowing that with a felony conviction I would be disbarred from the State Bar of Texas, I voluntarily resigned to indicate I would not contest my disbarment.

The final few days passed swiftly. Mary and I cherished every moment. She would remain in her apartment with

Muppet, our cat, to keep her company. She would also begin a sales job with Dover Homes in late January. It was a bittersweet time as the day of separation and my entry into an unknown world rapidly drew closer.

On Thursday afternoon, January 2, Mary and I flew to El Paso, rented a car and drove to the Days Inn where I had made a reservation. Seeing the parking lot full of eighteen-wheelers, Mary gasped, "We are not staying here?"

"Where else are we going to go?" I responded. "This is fairly close to Ft. Bliss, and we can't afford a nicer place. We just ought to try and make the best of it."

With resignation in her voice, she agreed. That evening, we drove to the Great American Land & Cattle Company steakhouse that overlooked the lights of El Paso and Juarez, Mexico, for a quiet, sad dinner. As we returned to our room, we realized that where we were staying was not important. Being together was all that mattered.

The next morning after breakfast we made the painful journey to Ft. Bliss and the Federal Prison Camp, where I became Inmate #53177-079.

Nine

Un Dia a la Vez
(One Day at a Time)

A GLARE OF LIGHT IN MY EYES, a tapping on my mattress near my shoulder, and a voice saying, "Moore, Moore, get up," jolted me upright from a deep sleep. A hack looked at me from two feet away. He shone a flashlight in my eyes and whispered that I had to get up to begin my A&O duties.

It was very early Saturday morning, my second day at Federal Prison Camp El Paso (FPC ELP), January 4, 1992.

Just like in the free world, weekends were non-working days for most of the inmates except those in food service. The most fortunate inmates were those who had visits from family and friends from 8 a.m. until 3 p.m. They could eat lunch together by purchasing a meal from a pre-approved vendor. Those who had no visitors had free time. However, for an A&O, our duties continued. So, I would be picking up trash and butts and cleaning the bathroom.

Preparing for the windy cold weather, I used an extra pair of socks for gloves and wrapped a towel around my neck as a scarf. I wore two T-shirts and two regular shirts under my windbreaker, but the wind pierced right through anyway.

During our first morning "butt pickup," we joined three other A&Os who had arrived several days earlier. One tall, balding, dignified-looking man, Curtis, was from Houston. We walked around the buildings and the mile-long dilapidated asphalt service road inside the camp, picking up trash as we talked. The hacks watched us constantly to make sure we kept working.

As the day wore on, I met more inmates in Franklin, all the while being careful not to ask why they were here. Phil and I continued to talk on our rounds. I learned that he would only be here for five months and would then serve five months in the El Paso Halfway House. He didn't like the length of his sentence, but it sure sounded better than 24 months. Living in El Paso, his wife Betty and two of his three grown sons who also lived there could visit him every weekend until he got out. How fortunate! I was already homesick for Mary...and I had just arrived!

Sunday morning, my third day, I was awakened again by a hack's flashlight. After I completed my A&O chores, Max invited me to go to chapel with him. He told me that a Protestant service would be held in a building near the warehouse.

About 30 inmates had crowded into the small room set up for the service. Even though the room had no heater, within minutes the windows had completely fogged up. I was the only newcomer in the crowd and, when requested, introduced myself.

As soon as everyone began singing the hymn "Majesty," I knew something powerful was happening. I could feel the presence of the Spirit in the singing. As I listened to the chaplain's sermon based on John 11, the death of Lazarus, I focused on the words of the Gospel. The more I thought about it, the more I realized why I was present that morning.

Lazarus was a symbol for me. I had thought that losing all my businesses, my marriage, and my home was punishment enough. But bad stuff kept coming and coming—relentlessly, unendingly. Prison wasn't the end of my trials. My bankruptcy proceeding was still pending, plus I had that blasted tax case. Both of those would be waiting for me when I got home and could resume fighting them. I would be returning as a convicted felon. That would change everything for me. It was scary. Could I handle it?

As those thoughts churned in my mind, the chaplain spoke of the need for Lazarus to be dead in order for Christ to bring him back to life. In that moment I realized that the old Harvin had to die in order for a new Harvin to emerge. That is, it had to get bad enough for me to understand that nothing could be the same—not ever. Just a little pain and discomfort wouldn't accomplish God's plan for me. My soul had to be purged! I had to "get it" that He had a completely new purpose for my life. Mary had often said that I had to go to prison not just to be punished, but to discover my true purpose. That morning, sitting in that service with those inmates, the room vibrating with their inspired singing, I knew she was right. Lazarus had to die in order to be raised. And so must I.

During communion, as we sang "I am Covered Over," I felt like I hadn't felt in years—I had been touched by the Spirit. As I walked out, a second realization dawned: God would have something important for me to do after my time in El Paso. Indeed, He wasn't through with me. Feeling rejuvenated, I knew this prison experience was not the end.

Arriving at the cafeteria, Max and I were last in line for what the Bureau of Prisons (BOP) called "brunch," which certainly didn't measure up to the fare, much less the service, that one could expect at an actual restaurant.

Each day, now with blistered feet, I walked gingerly along the asphalt road, picking up butts and trash. Looking eastward, I could see the familiar orange planes of Southwest Airlines approaching El Paso International Airport. I would be instantly transported to a tropical island for a beach vacation—my escape without escaping. Playing this mental game became a habit for me.

Evenings were the only time I could write Mary a letter, so I began to search for a quieter and more comfortable place than Franklin, with its high noise level and lack of seating except my bunk or metal chair. The dining room across the grounds from Franklin was open in the evenings, but with two TVs in opposite corners of the room, it was also noisy. I had tried the library—a tiny room tucked within the main building where the cafeteria and most administrative offices were—but it had only a few chairs. I gave up and just wrote her from my bunk.

During lunch on Monday, I noticed that a BOP van had pulled up near the R&D trailer and unloaded eight men handcuffed and chained together. As I stared at this unexpected sight, I asked Curtis what was happening.

"They're being transferred here from another prison," he replied.

"But why are they handcuffed and chained?"

He shrugged. "That's the way all prisoners are transported."

"Even to a camp—handcuffed and chained? I don't believe it."

"You'll get used to it. And if you should ever go out, it'll be that way."

"You're kidding?! I self-surrendered. I'm not going to run away."

"Well, the BOP doesn't trust anyone, even you, once they lock you up. The only time you'll go out without handcuffs and chains is if you get a furlough or go to a halfway house, but that's it."

It hit me. "So, if I get called back to testify in Houston, I go out that way?"

"Yep, 'cept the U.S. Marshals come and get you. You'll be handcuffed, and they'll put a chain around your waist, and the handcuffs will be locked to the chain. That's called 'going out on a writ,' and it might take several days to get you back to Houston."

I shuddered. How grim.

We were permitted to use the telephones when the afternoon count cleared, usually around 4:30 p.m., until lights out at around 11 p.m. Even though all calls had to be "collect" (a very expensive way to call), there was always a problem using the phones. We had only one, located at the end of our floor that housed seventy inmates. But that phone didn't work! Actually, there were only eight working phones scattered across the camp for the use of 300 inmates. Calls were officially limited to fifteen minutes, but inmates from the El Paso area, in particular, widely disregarded this rule and the hacks did nothing about it. Those were "local" calls, subject only to a small toll charge.

It infuriated me that the hacks wouldn't enforce the time limit. With my A&O duties, I couldn't stand in line for long periods waiting to use the phone because a hack would call me out to pick up trash or clean a bathroom, and I'd lose my place.

The cold grew bitter quickly. My fifth day, an inmate who worked in the warehouse offered to "find" a wool cap for me in return for a pack of cigarettes. My new friends had told me that the inmates in the warehouse unpacked newly arrived clothing. One could get me a cap—for a small quid pro quo, of course. Evidently every society, no matter how small or disenfranchised, has a "black" market.

That evening I skipped dinner in order to call Mary. Missing dinner didn't matter because I accomplished my first priority of talking with her. I longed to hear her voice and to know that she was okay. Plus, I had purchased a jar of peanut butter, granola bars, and grapefruit juice at the commissary, so I had something to eat.

As the end of my first week approached, I was still worn out after each long day from my A&O duties, aggravated because I still had no winter jacket. The stress of coping in this new environment was also wearing. When I went to bed at night, I quickly fell asleep in spite of my thin, sagging mattress.

Lost in a dream of being any place but here, I heard, somewhere in the distance, shouting. It got louder. I rolled over; but the sounds grew even louder and closer. I slowly lifted my head toward the noise coming from outside, reached for my glasses and looked through the window behind my locker toward the main building. Floodlights outlined the buildings, making them gray against the dark sky. I slowly recognized that people were running around, shouting, screaming, throwing things at each other. The entire mass of people moved back and forth as the battle raged. Soon, flashing red lights of law-enforcement vehicles pulled up near the battlefield. Guards jumped out and approached the crowd. I froze, staring in disbelief at what was unfolding before me.

Oh no, I thought. Surely it's not a prison riot. So soon after I've gotten here? What am I going to do? Who's out there? Who's fighting whom and why? Will it spread to Franklin? Oh, please God, don't let it be a riot, please. I buried my head in my pillow and held my breath.

Suddenly, from another direction, I heard laughing and talking. Down the hall, a group of inmates approached the bunks. Without moving a muscle, I listened intently.

Then, I learned what had happened. After the lights were turned off, it had begun to snow. A large number of inmates had been watching a movie in the main building, with permission. After the movie, as they walked back to the barracks and saw snow on the ground, a snowball fight ensured. Just like kids, they took this unexpected opportunity for a little midnight fun.

After hearing this explanation, my whole body relaxed. I chuckled silently as I overheard one inmate say to another, "I haven't seen so much 'snow' since I was busted in Eagle Pass" (snow being slang for cocaine). Relieved, I soon fell asleep.

A new inmate's most anxiously awaited appointment is the first one with the case manager (CM) who monitors his file and progress. In theory, the CM "helps" prepare him for an eventual return to the free world. Each inmate also has a counselor (though definitely not a psychologist) who helps him "cope" during prison life. From the moment an inmate arrives, he focuses on how quickly he can legitimately (in most cases) get out.

The first meeting with my CM, Ms. Storey, occurred about ten days after my arrival. I had already learned enough to hustle over early to stand outside her office. Although I wasn't first in line, I was early enough to see her without waiting several hours (but I always carried a book in my back pocket to read just in case).

Once inside, my first questions were about when I would be eligible for a furlough and how much halfway-house time I would get. She would not answer these questions until I'd been there at least ninety days. But she did say that my mandatory release date—the day I would be freed from incarceration from either the camp or the halfway house—would be September 30, 1993, provided I earned the entire good-time credit of fifty-four days a year.

"Since this is leap year, why wouldn't it be September 29th?" I asked wryly. Ms. Storey failed to see my logic or appreciate my tongue-in-cheek humor.

She gave me the form on which to list twelve possible visitors, the maximum number allowed any inmate. Each member of my family counted as one. The form required their full names, dates of birth, and social security numbers so that the BOP could do a background check. No convicted felon could visit me. And, until the completed form had been processed and approved, no one could visit.

Ms. Storey also gave me a list of precise rules to follow if I wanted someone to send civilian clothes that I could wear in my leisure time. Those rules covered the exact types, colors, sizes and amount of clothing; if the specs were not followed exactly, the whole shipment would be sent back. She also reminded me that no one could send stamps or hardcover books because hallucinogens could be injected into the glue.

The final point she raised was the restitution I owed. She told me that as soon as I got a job, $25 per quarter would be deducted from my pay and sent to the court for application toward the amount of $573,925.83, regardless which of the four pay scales at the camp (Grade One, 12 cents an hour; Grade Two, 17 cents an hour; Grade Three, 29 cents an hour; and Grade Four, 40 cents an hour) I was paid.

After I shared all of this information with Mary that evening, she excitedly told me her news: my good friend and attorney Raymond Kerr and his wife Nancy had given her a Southwest Airlines ticket to El Paso—she was coming to see me the following weekend!

The next morning I told Phil that Mary would be coming to El Paso. As he puffed on a cigarette he said, "We live just fifteen minutes from the camp. My wife Betty would love to have Mary stay with her. She needs the companionship."

"Phil, are you serious?" I asked, elated at the possibility.

"Absolutely. I'll tell her when I call her tonight. She'll love having company all weekend, especially when she's not here visiting me."

"That's wonderful. I know Mary will be thrilled to have her company, too, and a place to stay."

Betty happily agreed to host Mary on what, as it turned out, was a long weekend that included the Martin Luther King, Jr. holiday. What a godsend for us!

As I heard of a possible job opening, I filled out the application form as soon as possible. But I was rejected as a tile setter, the librarian and for several other jobs.

One of the inmates, an assistant cook named Gordo, was a mountain of a man-child with an infectious laugh, a mischievous sense of humor, and an ability to poke fun at the staff—even to their faces. That night he asked, "Harv, would you like to work in the kitchen?"

"Yeah, Gordo. Anything inside would be great," I smiled.

"Well, one of the assistant cooks is leaving, so I'll mention you to the cook foreman." He directed me to fill out the application and promised to ask the foreman to request me.

"We'll give it our best shot, Harv. Just be ready to join the team—my team," he said as he grinned and turned, laughing "Ha ha ha ha ha!" as he schlepped his 290-pound, six-foot-one frame down the hall to his room. Gordo knew the "system," having been "down" four times before. So I expected to get this job.

Saturday morning, January 18, I woke up at 5:45 very excited. Mary would arrive with Betty at 8 a.m. for her first visit. Immediately after eating a cinnamon roll and drinking coffee, the hack told me to clean the Visitors' room, which was also our large dining room. It was just across the hall from the small dining room where the cafeteria line was. I was happy to do that especially because of the day's icy, blustery weather. Finishing the task, I walked back to Franklin to wait with Phil for the loudspeaker announcement summoning me to the Visitors' room.

The wait nearly exasperated me. At 8:40, Phil was called, but I wasn't. That seemed strange since Betty and Mary were together. On weekends, there was always a 9 a.m. count. At 8:55, I finally found a hack and asked him to call the Visitor's room to see if Mary was there. "She's there," he said, "but it's too close to Count Time for you to go over."

"I can run over there before they call the count," I pleaded, but he refused.

"What?" I felt my face flush. "They fouled it up over there."

"Yeah," he agreed, sensing my anger, "and I'm sorry, but you'll just have to wait."

I stayed by my bunk until the count cleared at 9:25, then rushed over to the Visitors' room. The hack at the door told me to empty my pockets. I unloaded a Chapstick, address book and $2.50 in change.

He glanced at the little pile. "You can't take anything in but $2 in quarters. Put that stuff back in your locker and come back."

"What's wrong with Chapstick, an address book, and two-fifty?!" I stammered.

"It's the rules," he said nonchalantly.

I had never heard of that rule or seen it posted. Fuming, I shoved everything back in my pocket, ran to Franklin and my second-floor bunk, crammed the items into my locker, and rushed back. All of this nonsense had cost us one precious hour.

During a visit, the rules permitted only a short kiss and embrace when an inmate greeted and said goodbye to his guest. Over the course of our visit, Mary and I stepped outside onto the porch twice for fresh air, but we were never out of sight of a hack. Other than that, we never left the table with Phil and Betty. I held Mary's hand the whole time. The hacks continually monitored the room for inappropriate conduct. If they observed bad behavior, the visitor would be removed and punishment inflicted on the inmate. Except for the coming-and-going kiss and embrace, holding hands above the table was "it" for everyone.

Nearly all the visitors that day were families of the Hispanic inmates. Their children, dressed to the nines, were extremely well behaved. It felt like a big family reunion, although the hacks discouraged any visiting between groups.

Sunday morning, Phil and I were both called for our visits at 8:20. Since camp rules permitted visitors to attend church services with their inmate host, Mary and I went to the Protestant service where she met Max and his wife, Linda.

Monday, even though a holiday, was a regular workday for most inmates, particularly A&Os. I doubly enjoyed her visit that day because I was excused from picking up cigarette butts—at least until after she left at 3 p.m.

During the visit, we finalized my list of potential visitors so she would know who to ask for the sensitive personal information required. I also gave her a detailed list of civilian clothing; I wanted what she sent to be exactly correct. As 3 p.m. approached, we said a sad goodbye, not knowing when she could return.

On January 21, after 18 long days of A&O duty, I began work as an assistant cook. What a huge relief! I would earn 17 cents an hour. Imagine being so excited about getting a job, any job, and being paid 17 cents an hour! Compared to my first job 44 years earlier at Minimax Grocery Store, where I had earned 35 cents an hour, I was losing ground. The prison world was upside down. But at least I could see things getting better.

My first day as an assistant cook, however, was an eye-opener. I worked from 4:30 a.m. until 12:45 p.m. when the shift ended. I sat down only twice—for breakfast and lunch. I made three trips outside to the lower-level cooler to carry up 50-pound bags of potatoes to peel, then took them to the slicer. Then I had to clean the equipment. Next, we made two 50-gallon kettles of soup. Finally, I mopped the floor— the first of three times that day—and carried most of the dirty equipment and utensils to the dish room. It was hard, physical labor.

I was exhausted at the end of my shift, exacerbated by still having to wear my heavy, oversized work boots. I fell asleep on my bunk as soon as I lay down.

Having a regular job made it easier to call Mary every night; no longer would I get yanked out of the phone line for A&O duty. Because it was so expensive, we talked only a few minutes. Thankfully, I could vent my frustration and anger toward the BOP in those calls without fear of reprisal or being "snitched" out to a hack. She would just listen and calm me down.

My next visitor was Jack Webb, a Houston lawyer, who stopped by on his way to Los Angeles on business. (And no, he wasn't the one who portrayed Joe "Just the facts, Ma'am" Friday on the TV series Dragnet.) Any lawyer could visit an inmate without going through hoops that regular visitors endured. Lawyers simply had to call and say we'd be discussing legal matters, and they were allowed to visit any time of day. Jack seemed shocked at the reality of seeing me there, but his visit really cheered me up. Over the next several months, he and his wife Diane gave Mary two plane tickets to visit me—visits that would not have been possible without their generosity.

Near the end of February, I got very good news: Raymond Kerr reported that Nancy had paid the $400,000 balance due the RTC under the settlement agreement. I had left Houston worried that I would end up with a $1.15 million RTC judgment against me unless she used the funds segregated as the income from her separate property. Nancy was infuriated that she had to pay for that liability. But had she not paid it, Raymond was convinced the government would have tried to collect the $1.15 million from her. I was relieved to have at least one less problem awaiting my return home.

Raymond also said that Nancy had settled her side of the tax case with the IRS. I groaned, "Raymond, we didn't owe the IRS anything! When I get back, I'm gonna fight them to my last breath. We don't owe them one dime. Why did she settle?"

"Probably just to get it over with and get rid of your problems," he said.

In mid March, Mimi, Harvin and Marian flew to El Paso to visit me. Mimi and Marian seemed very uncomfortable in the prison setting but were glad to see that I was well adjusted. In contrast, Harvin seemed more at ease, though I suspected he was also somewhat uncomfortable. In declining health, my father was confined to a wheelchair and couldn't travel. I worried continually whether he would live until my release because the warden would not have let me attend his funeral.

A month or so after I arrived, an upper bunk next to Max's became vacant. I asked the hack if I could move. He agreed, and I relocated my stuff to a new location amidst a handful of white-collar criminals, arsonists, illegal animal importers, and drug-conspiracy members. Now, on the east side of Franklin, the rising sun would shine through my window just above my locker and usher in each new day. Residing in the next bunk was Bob, the food-service clerk. In that job, he prepared the schedules for three shifts, the payroll, the food ordering and purchasing, and all other food-service paperwork. Typing was an essential part of the job. And, I learned, he would soon leave for a halfway house.

As his departure day approached, he told me that since I could type and understood how the kitchen worked, he'd recommend me to the Food Service Administrator as his successor. I thanked him and said a silent prayer of gratitude for having taken that typing class at Lanier Junior High School and maintaining the skill.

A week before Bob left, the administrator called the food-service workers together in the kitchen and announced Bob's departure. He thanked him for his work and announced that I would be the new clerk. Just like that. No one talked to me about it except Bob, but I realized that the white-collar inmates did the office jobs at the camp. Their successors were almost always recommended by the inmate leaving. The inmates knew who could do the job, and the staff usually relied on their suggestions.

Until this announcement was made, however, I didn't let myself think about how happy I'd be to leave the cook line and settle into a job I could handle. I was immediately transferred into the office to work with Bob for his remaining days. I'd be using a computer with a word-processing program. Even though it was a generation or two behind the current technology, still it was a computer. And my pay would jump to $.40 an hour. Not counting visits with Mary, family and friends, this was my best day yet at El Paso.

Beckworth, the assistant food service administrator, was one of the few BOP staffers liked and respected by the inmates. About six-foot-two and 215 pounds of muscle, this 30-something man still carried himself like a college-football linebacker. After college, he coached a while before joining the BOP. A Type-A personality, he could be gruff, but he didn't ask any of us to do something that he himself wouldn't do. He evenhandedly doled out the work and the criticism. He wasn't burdened with an inflated sense of self-importance, either. People simply liked working for him.

Our 10' x 15' windowless office, filled with three desks and chairs, along with filing cabinets, was located outside the back door of the kitchen. In the winter, it was frigid because the warden would not permit use of a space heater. The solid-wood door remained locked when Beckworth and Robles, the administrators, were away. The space was claustrophobic unless you could control that fear. When the camp had regional BOP staff visitors, and both administrators had to leave, I would be locked inside the office—a prison within a prison. I hated that, but fortunately I never had an emergency, and they usually returned within an hour or so.

Ten

A Change of Plans

At our next scheduled meeting, Ms. Storey explained Camp rules regarding furloughs and halfway-house assignments. Though she and the staff could recommend furloughs, the warden had the final say. He also had authority over the number of days an inmate would get at the halfway house. Clearly, he had a lot of power over our lives.

To get a furlough, an inmate had to have a "clean" record without any "shots" (extra work assignments for improper behavior). He had to have been at the camp at least six months and be within twelve months of his mandatory release date. By the fall, I would be eligible for a thirty-hour furlough (Saturday morning until Sunday afternoon) to be spent only in El Paso. Shortly after that, I would be eligible for a five-day furlough to go home. The BOP intended this visit to "strengthen family ties, interview for a job, and begin reconnecting to your community". Then Ms. Storey dropped a bombshell. She wouldn't recommend a furlough for me if I'd be released to a fiancée. Being released to a wife was okay, but not otherwise.

What kind of rule is that? I thought. I'm fifty-four, never had a substance abuse problem, and can handle the ups and downs of life. The camp knows I'll do what I'm supposed to. After all, I self-surrendered. I certainly don't need a wife to meet me at the gate.

That evening I called Mary to share this news. It really didn't surprise her because I had found a number of things frustrating and illogical.

Given all that, I asked Mary if she'd consider letting the chaplain marry us here. Even though Mary had wanted to get married sooner rather than later, I had suggested that by waiting until I got out, we could have a "normal" wedding. She eventually agreed with that. Now, I was asking her to reconsider and do it sooner.

After thinking about it for a few days, Mary agreed for us to be married at the camp and suggested August 23rd. Her parents' anniversary was that day and she considered their marriage the best of anyone she had ever known. I agreed to the date.

Mary began doing the paperwork and getting the approvals required by the BOP, the U.S. Department of Justice (DOJ), and finally the warden. Among other things, Mary had to write the warden and ask permission to marry me. Mary asked her sister Nancy to stand with her at the service and I asked my brother, Barry. Since Nancy was not on my approved Visitor List, I asked the chaplain to obtain special permission for her to attend, which was granted.

Meanwhile, my life settled into a routine as I mastered my food-service position. It was a very good job, as prison jobs go. Being the only inmate in the office was almost like being in the free world. Mr. Robles and Beckworth constantly came in and out of the office as they oversaw the work of the cook foremen and the ordering, inventorying, and scheduling. Daily, I prepared the inmate work schedule for the following day and posted it in all three living areas. I prepared purchase orders for the food and requests for equipment purchases. Weekly, I gave a safety talk to all three shifts. Monthly, I prepared the inmate payroll, which was approved by Beckworth. If money was left in the budget for bonuses, they'd tell me how to apply it. The lead cooks and I invariably would get a bonus each month, but they tried to distribute bonus money as far and wide as possible.

A few inmates assigned to food service turned out to be thieves (imagine that!) and stole food to sell to their hungry friends. The cook foremen were constantly on guard against this behavior, particularly when we served menudo, steaks, or chicken on the bone. When caught, the inmate would get fired. However, inmates working there were permitted to take a little food back to their rooms for themselves. Recognizing that these were some of the toughest jobs at camp—long, hard hours plus working every weekend and holiday—the staff cut us a little slack.

At the end of May, Phil departed for the halfway house in El Paso, but thanks to our friendship and his and Betty's generosity, Mary would continue to be welcomed each time she came to see me.

One day I had a surprise visit from two men—from the Houston office of the FBI. I was immediately excused from work to talk with them in the library. In that small room— which was unoccupied during the workday—we pulled our three chairs together and began the interview about another loan investigation at MSA.

After about an hour, they were satisfied I'd told them all I knew and they left. Some of my co-workers in food service were impressed that the FBI had come to FPC ELP rather than making me return to Houston. I didn't care about impressing anyone; I was just thankful they hadn't hauled me back to Houston on a Writ.

I knew that had I gone out on a Writ, the U.S. Marshals would have taken me off my job in handcuffs locked to a chain around my waist and transported me by car or van back to Houston. It was never a one-day trip as they usually picked up inmates from other prisons along the way. Nights in transit would be spent in holding cells or local jails with all manner of criminals. Mary would not know that I had been taken, nor where I was going. When the interrogation was completed, I would be returned to FPC ELP the same way, and only then could I let her know what had happened. Some inmates taken out on Writs didn't return for a month or more. Since they were in transit all of that time, the inmates referred to it as "diesel therapy".

It took about a month for the DOJ to determine it had no objection to our getting married. Soon after, the warden gave his consent. Our wedding was scheduled, as planned, for August 23, which was also the day before my birthday. I knew I'd never forget our anniversary.

Weddings at the camp were most unusual. My new friends were excited for me. Mary and Nancy arrived Sunday morning. I had ironed my khaki pants, but when I put on a shirt, Ric, a nearby neighbor, told me I didn't look sharp enough and insisted I wear his Ralph Lauren khaki shirt, which matched my pants. He even ironed it again to make sure it looked perfect.

Mary wore a white-cotton pleated dress, overlaid at the waist with an embroidered skirt that extended below the knee. She had on white hose and white pumps. Betty had made a silk flower corsage for her hair and a silk flower bouquet for her to hold. To all who may have been looking, they knew something unique was about to transpire at FPC ELP.

Mary, Nancy and I walked to the chapel for the church service at 10 a.m. The chaplain introduced them to the worshippers and told a Swedish joke, not realizing that Mary's last name "Jensen" was Danish. Then he invited everyone to return at noon for our wedding. Afterward, we returned to the visitor patio and met Barry as he arrived.

I'd invited a number of my inmate friends to come, especially those whose spouses were visiting that day. In addition, I had purchased photo tickets at the commissary. Photographs were to be taken only by a certain inmate who used the camp's 35mm camera. Then a staff person would take the film into El Paso for processing.

A few minutes before noon, our bridal party headed for the chapel, followed by several groups of friends. The chaplain met us at the door and walked with us to the front of the room. We stood facing the audience as friends came in and sat down—between forty and fifty people. Sean, who lived in the bunk next to me, played the keyboard, but not the "Wedding March". After all, the bride wasn't walking up the aisle; she was already in place! Another inmate's wife, who was choral director of the annual Viva El Paso pageant, sang "One Hand, One Heart" from West Side Story and "Through the Eyes of Love" from Ice Castles. This magical music carried us to a different place, making us wonder how such inspiration and beauty could find its way inside a prison.

The chaplain conducted the service facing us while we faced the gathering. He said that God, in creating Eve, did not take something from Adam's head or from his feet, since

He intended that neither would be inferior nor superior to the other. Instead, he took something from Adam's chest, a rib, because it was from the middle of his body and a part that covered and protected the heart. As he said that, Mary squeezed my hand and we smiled at each other.

At the back door, two hacks stood quietly watching everything. Indeed, no one had been aware of their presence before or during the ceremony until one of their radios squawked.

At the conclusion of the ceremony, the chaplain asked us to stand at the door so everyone could greet us as they left the room. Several guys bravely kissed Mary on the cheek as the hacks turned the other way. One inmate gave Mary a hand-colored handkerchief while another had drawn a cartoon of us getting married, portraying Mary in a long wedding dress and me in prison stripes with a ball and chain attached to my ankle. It had been signed by a number of inmates. The hacks even let Mary take these treasures home with her.

After the receiving line played out and a few photos of the wedding party taken, we walked back to our patio table for the rest of our visiting time. Barry and I stepped inside the main building to buy soft drinks. While we were gone, Mary unwrapped two honey buns she had bought that morning at the vending machine. One represented the bride's cake and one the groom's cake. She had mashed them together and placed a tiny, plastic bride and groom in the center. The photographer was so impressed with Mary's ingenuity that he took a photo and didn't require a "ticket" for that one.

All too soon, visitation period ended. Mary had to leave with Nancy and Barry while I returned to Franklin. One of the hacks who had stood at the back of the chapel kiddingly asked, "Where are you going on your honeymoon?"

"Franklin," I said glumly.

Later that evening, Roy came by my bunk and said, "I've never seen two people look at each other like you all did. It was just unbelievable the love that shines between you two. I've never witnessed a wedding quite like that before, and not just because it was in prison. You have something very special."

Touched with emotion, all I could say was a simple, heartfelt, "Yes, we do. Thank you."

The next day, Monday, August 24, was a regular workday, although it was my fifty-fifth birthday. Except for a handful of inmate friends sharing cookies after supper and reading treasured mail from family and friends, I spent it like any other day at the camp.

My focus quickly turned to requesting my first furlough September 19-20, to be with Mary for thirty hours. I filled out the forms and gave them to Ms. Storey, confident the furlough would be granted. Meanwhile, Mary arranged her visit in September to coincide with that furlough date and made a reservation at a downtown hotel. No Days Inn this time; this would be our honeymoon.

Around the first of September, a new warden was assigned to FPC ELP. Everyone was anxious about how he would run the prison. By Thursday, September 17, I hadn't heard anything about my furlough request. I told Mary I had a funny feeling about it, that she'd better bring regular "visiting" clothes, too. Ms. Storey was off Friday and Saturday, so Friday morning, I asked Beckworth if he would call a staff person to learn whether I had been granted the furlough.

He did and was told the new warden had denied it. Beckworth said I could go get the particulars from Ms. Storey's supervisor, which I did immediately. He told me the warden had turned down all furlough requests due to "paperwork problems." But, he said he'd try to get one for me the following weekend.

"Mr. White," I said, fighting to remain calm, "my wife has gotten off work to come out here this weekend and is already on the plane. It's a wasted trip and wasted money. She can only get one weekend off a month. So no, I don't want a furlough next weekend."

I walked back to work, seething inside and thinking, I've followed all the rules, never had a problem of any kind, and filled out the request correctly. I am—by the camp's own policies—absolutely entitled to that furlough. But I knew I had to control my emotions. I wasn't a free citizen; I was a prisoner, there to be punished.

Still agitated, to burn it off I started walking briskly around the track, my mind drifting back to the day the government had taken over MSA and my punishment had really begun—a day when I faced the cruel reality that everything would be different.

Eleven

It's No Country Club

Suddenly, I heard someone call my name. It grew louder. "Harvin, Harvin!"

I stopped walking and turned to see Tito, the "salad man" on one of the kitchen shifts, hurrying toward me. A large middle-aged man, he was breathing heavily as his voice rose in anger. "Have you heard what the new warden just did?"

"No," I replied as he caught up.

"He just banned leaving the camp after supper for all inmates, so we can't continue our computer class, that SOB!"

"He did what?" I asked, staring.

"Yeah. Even those not taking classes are stunned."

Tito shook his head. He was working toward a degree at El Paso Community College's satellite location on Fort Bliss, outside the prison camp. This disappointment hit him hard. We walked slowly back into Franklin, talked a little longer to calm down, and contemplated what the new warden would do next.

We found out all too soon: He decided we should not wear civilian clothes on weekends or during leisure time. We were ordered to box them up and mail them home. Compliance was enforced by the hacks who searched our lockers frequently, though randomly. We now had to wear our blue prison uniforms at all times.

This new warden had a habit of periodically touring the compound with an entourage of eight to ten staff people. After the first such procession, the Hispanic inmates began calling him "Santa Anna," the Mexican general defeated by Sam Houston at the battle of San Jacinto in 1836, which secured Texas' independence from Mexico.

I guess to be certain that everyone knew he was the boss, Santa Anna had the vending machines in the large dining room removed. With that, some inmates came unglued. They plotted revenge with the undivided focus of a bull speared by a picador. Interestingly, staff members were just as disgruntled with that decision.

Santa Anna then decreed that all inmates who worked in food service would henceforth live in the main building, Hueco, whose lower level had four-man and eight-man rooms that offered a little more privacy than the barracks. I, however, didn't want to move away from my close friends or adjust to new roommates. I objected to Beckworth, but to no avail.

When I walked into my new room with my belongings, Joel, the lead cook, handed me an apple, banana and some dip with chips, welcoming me into my new "family". Joel had a leonine head covered with thick, coal-black hair and greenish-gray eyes. He had an intimidating presence.

Back in Houston, Mary learned that the tenants at our home in Seabrook were moving in October '92. My mandatory release date was not until next September 30, but I was hopeful of getting six months at a halfway house, typical for anyone with a sentence of two years or longer. By getting a job after I got to the halfway house, I could go home every weekend. Conceivably, I could be coming home as early as March. Mary decided to move in so she would be settled and my transition home would be easier.

Now eligible for a five-day furlough, I wanted to use it to help her move. I requested a furlough for the latter part of October.

One Sunday in mid-October, Ms. Storey called me to her office. With Mr. White present, she asked, "Have you seen the article in today's El Paso newspaper that mentioned you would be a government witness in an upcoming fraud trial in Houston?"

"Yes, I have. Why do you ask?"

"Does it give you any concern?" she asked.

"No. Why...because I'm a government witness?"

"Yes."

"No, I haven't had a problem and I don't expect to," I said matter-of-factly.

White interjected, "We've taken in a lot of new inmates from higher levels of security, and you should be careful. If anyone or anything threatens you, the camp will protect you by moving you immediately to another facility."

Without hesitation, I replied, "Mr. White, I'm well-situated here, I've been here long enough to know a lot of people, I have a good job, and I don't expect trouble of any kind."

"Good," they said in unison. White added, "But at the slightest sign, you tell us. We don't want you to get hurt."

"I appreciate that, and I'll let you know if I feel uneasy about anything."

I walked back to my room, suddenly feeling vulnerable. I hadn't thought about it before, but now I couldn't stop.

That evening, after dark, I noticed a clipping newly tacked on the Hueco bulletin board, right at the entry door. It was the article about the Houston trial of Joe Russo in which I would be a corroborating witness for the government. Some inmate had posted it and highlighted my name in yellow. Surprised, but not enough to lose my wits, I tore it off and threw it away. Unconvincingly, I told myself to quit thinking about it.

My senses were on high alert for the next few days, although I tried to hide my nervousness. No one said anything to me about the article, and I never felt threatened.

Near the end of October, Max left FPC ELP. I was happy for him, but I certainly would miss his warm, caring and pleasant friendship.

By this time, my five-day furlough request had been processed and was again...rejected. No reason this time. As a result, Mary would have to manage the move alone.

"If they aren't going to grant me a furlough, why can't they tell me upfront?" I asked Ms. Storey. "That way, I won't get my hopes up." She could offer no reply.

With Ms. Storey's encouragement, however, I applied for another five-day furlough, this time over Christmas. She believed that by applying right away I'd get mine in before the crush of holiday-furlough applications. Also, the higher-ups might remember that they had turned me down twice and react differently this time.

At that meeting, she also told me the warden was no longer giving six months in the halfway house unless an inmate had a long sentence, say, more than five years. She thought I was still likely to get four months. If so, that meant going back to Houston on May 26, not as good as March but better than September. She also said that after being at the halfway house a while, I might get home confinement. Something to hope for!

Shortly after the first of November, my case manager informed me, "Moore, your Christmas furlough has been denied."

"Not again," I growled. "I don't understand. Why this time?"

She glanced at my file. "They said the money in your case was too big a factor."

"You know that more than 85 percent of the restitution has been paid and I am making regular payments toward the balance," I said. "In fact, I voluntarily raised my payment from $25 to $50 a quarter."

"Yes, I know...but they didn't consider that."

"What do you mean? They just ignore the facts to suit themselves?"

She shrugged nonchalantly.

My frustration and anger began to emerge. "I can't believe this! Will you give me a cop-out form so I can request a meeting with the warden about it? I've earned that furlough. What have they got against me?"

She handed me the B-9 form, which I filled out requesting a meeting and an explanation of why all of my furloughs had been denied. I knew it would take weeks to get an answer, but Santa Anna owed me one as he was granting furloughs regularly to other inmates.

Just prior to Thanksgiving, Joel had been working in the kitchen around the clock, primarily making pumpkin pies. On Wednesday night, he walked carefully into our room with a lump of something hidden under the windbreaker that was draped across his arm, and removed the jacket to unveil a whole pie.

"How in the world did you sneak that thing out?" I asked.

He grinned. "I made one for the lieutenant on duty and one for the hack in the control room."

This was Joel's "extra compensation" for the long hours, a treat for him and his roommates—not to be sold, of course—so it was unofficially overlooked.

On Thanksgiving, Mary arrived at 8 a.m. for our seven-hour visit. It was her first visit since September and would also be the last in the camp's large dining room. The remodeling of an abandoned chapel on Biggs Airfield had been completed, converting it into our Visitation room. Visits would move to that location for the balance of the weekend—except for Friday, a regular work day at FPC ELP—with inmates bused there in groups.

That evening, Joel and his shift prepared Thanksgiving dinner and served 445 meals. All 423 inmates were there along with some of the staff. No one missed this meal. And Joel said the Christmas "feast" would be just as good.

New offices for Food Service were under construction at the rear of the kitchen, but that project was, typically, way behind schedule. As a result, we continued working in our cramped office outside the kitchen. The place was unbearably cold in the winter. To make matters worse, Santa Anna wouldn't allow a space heater. Beckworth and Robles went in and out all the time, while I had to sit at my computer next to the door, bundled up in my winter jacket. I could barely keep my fingers warm enough to type. By the middle of the day, it usually warmed up enough to function normally, but those first few hours in the morning were agonizing.

Several days into December, one of my roommates left
for his halfway house, so the hacks let me move "downstairs"
to the lower bunk. Imagine! After eleven months to the day,
I would no longer have to climb up to my bed. Seniority had
its rewards, however trivial.

In mid-December, Robles asked, "Harv, what do you hear
about a food strike?"

"A what?" I didn't hear him clearly.

"I hear some inmates are planning a food strike. Are they?"

I assured him I had no idea.

"But you live with all these guys. What do you hear?"

"Absolutely nothing, Mr. Robles. Think about it: I work in
food service, I don't speak Spanish, and I'm 55 years old. I'm
not going to hear about any food strike."

He chuckled. "I guess you're right. But I heard one is
coming down. Won't be good for anyone involved."

"I guess not, but one thing I'm sure of—it's not about
the food."

"Thank goodness," he said as he turned back to his
paper work.

Food, or rather poor food, is a prominent cause of food
strikes in prisons. When that's the case, Food Service is casti-
gated by the BOP higher ups. However, it didn't surprise me
that something was cooking among the inmates because so
many were vehemently upset about the new warden's unwel-
come changes. Perhaps they weren't mature enough to know
they were powerless, that a strike would only hurt them. But
evidently, the staff was getting a hint of rising unrest. No
doubt, snitches lurked amongst the criminals.

Friday morning, December 18, as inmates were waiting
to be loaded on the yellow school buses for work at Fort

Bliss, Biggs Air Field, or UNICOR, I noticed that the BOP had also positioned its white bus on the road by the main building, Hueco. As the hacks called out names, the inmates were frisked, as usual, then directed to the yellow buses or, surprise, handcuffed and put on the BOP bus for a ride to the Hole (solitary confinement) at La Tuna. Six or seven were taken away, though none worked in food service. Out of 425 inmates, we served 122 at breakfast that morning, which was about average for a Friday. So the food strike never materialized. During the next few days, others were still being taken away because of their involvement. All in all, our camp lost about thirteen inmates.

On Friday, December 25, 1992, Mary arrived early at the Biggs Air Field Chapel. I was called at 7:35 and told that she was there. In fact, she was second in line. However, by the time the hacks arrived to check us out, load us into the van, drive us to the chapel and check us in, we'd wasted a lot of time. It was now 8:15. The room filled rapidly as the joyful and excited sounds of children and their families visiting their fathers to celebrate Christmas Day filled the room. It felt like a Christmas Day.

But around noon, a hack came over and said we had to leave. Mary jumped up and confronted him, boldly saying, "I've come nine-hundred miles to see my husband, and it's only the second time in three months."

She glared at him. I gulped. What would happen next?

Mary's assertive, spontaneous statement embarrassed the hack, but he said he had to enforce the camp's order that the first fifteen inmates to arrive that morning had to leave. My face flushed and I thought, Why penalize those who came less often and from the farthest distance? So I said to the hack, "The inmates from El Paso have visits every weekend, usually both days. Shouldn't they be the ones asked to leave?" It seemed to me a fairer way to handle the problem. The hack just shrugged. He hadn't made the decision, he was just enforcing it. Well, Merry Christmas to you too! The day's visit was over.

That evening, I found the duty officer and stated my case. He, too, apologized, and said that would not happen to us again. Mary also saw the chaplain after I had left and he intervened on our behalf with the duty officer.

As a sort of "Christmas bonus," early the next morning the toilets across the hall from my room overflowed. Raw sewage flowed into the hall and threatened the rooms, including mine. What a stinking and slimy mess! Realizing that the brown sludge was headed toward my room, I slammed the door, waking up my three roommates. Strings of Spanish expletives filled the air, mostly directed at me. As the men came to their senses, they directed their anger toward the brown stuff and the prison in general. We quickly jammed towels under the door, but not in time to prevent a couple of inches of watery fecal matter from covering the floor in our room. It took all of the inmates on our hallway several hours to clean up the mess.

Despite this, Mary and I enjoyed visiting for two full days, and Barry joined us on Sunday. Their departures provided another bittersweet moment, and a reminder that I still lived in a very different world.

Shortly after the first of the year, the warden ordered that all room doors be removed, making it easier for the hacks to look in and see what was going on. It seemed to me they walked in whenever they pleased, usually unannounced, so why remove the doors? However, we had to live with less privacy and, worse, more noise from the hallways—the telephones, washers and dryers were just around the corner from our room.

Several weeks later, the toilets backed up again and raw sewage flowed rapidly into our rooms because, of course, we had no doors. We used our blankets and towels to form a dam at the doorway, but it was of little help. It was a much more disgusting septic-malfunction experience than the previous one.

Early in January, Mary finally told me that her financial situation was desperate. She had not wanted to add her burden on top of mine and had tried to cope alone. But she was scared and felt more isolated than ever. Even though still working, money was scarce. With the title company having never honored its agreement to pay me a consulting fee, and no rental income from our home in Seabrook, Mary couldn't pay the mortgage or the other bills. She was stressed to the max!

I gave her a list of ten people I thought might lend us $200 a month. With their help, we could make the mortgage payment. I would pay them back when I returned home and got a job. I asked her to call and alert each one that I'd be calling them collect. I strongly believed I, not Mary, should ask them for financial help.

The following night, she told me the first person she called was Jerrol Springer, our friend and still my insurance agent. He told her to have me call him first and not to call anyone else until we had talked. Excitedly, I immediately called Jerrol. He answered the phone and, after exchanging pleasantries, got right to the point.

"What do you need?"

"We need some help in making our mortgage payment, Jerrol. If you could lend us $200 a month until I get back, that, with help from some other friends, will cover it. If you can do that, I'll pay you back when I get home and get a job."

Instantly, he said, "Have Mary call me in the morning at my office and tell me how much the payment is. I'll give her a check for the whole thing."

"But Jerrol, I can get others to chip in. I'm not asking you to do it all."

"I know you could, but this is what I want to do. Just tell her to call me and I'll give her the money. And I'll do that every month until you get back home and can get back to work. If y'all have other problems, then she can call them."

"Jerrol, that's too much! I…"

He cut in. "I'm going to do it, so take that off your list. Just get back as soon as you can."

"I will, Jerrol, and you'll never know how much we appreciate this."

I was overwhelmed, speechless. I had hoped he'd be willing to help along with others. This was more than any one person should do. What a friend!

I called Mary immediately to tell her this good news. As it sunk in, I could hear her softly crying with joy and relief. She wouldn't have to worry about the mortgage payment any more while I was gone. Amazingly, when times seem bleakest, someone shows up.

"No hay mal que por bien no venga." (There's nothing so bad that something good won't come from it.) Yes!

In response to my cop-out, in early March 1993 I was granted an audience with Estrada, one of the camp's two assistant wardens, to discuss the denial of my third furlough request. As I walked into his office, he motioned for me to sit in the wooden chair across from his desk.

"Moore, aren't you the one who went to Harvard?" he asked, his tone tinged with resentment.

"Yes sir," I answered. After graduating from Rice, I had attended Harvard Business School for one year before going to the University of Texas Law School.

"There was also a large money factor in your case. The warden doesn't want you to get a furlough because it might not look good in the community."

"Mr. Estrada, I was imprisoned because of financial fraud, so don't you think that denying me a furlough for the same reason might be punishing me for the same thing twice?"

He shrugged, and added that I had also obstructed justice.

"I did not!" I said immediately. "That is incorrect because that charge was dismissed. That shouldn't even be in my PSI, much less have anything to do with whether I get a furlough."

He listened, expressionless, but I could tell by looking into his cold eyes that he wouldn't let my words penetrate his consciousness. He'd already made up his mind. However, I needed to make one more point.

"Mr. Estrada, my file also reflects that 85 percent of the restitution has been paid and that I am also paying $50 a quarter toward the balance. Shouldn't that matter?"

"I'll look into it, but you're still not gonna get a furlough."

The meeting ended. Feeling frustrated and boiling mad, I left the room knowing I would get nothing more than the satisfaction of that one opportunity to state my case. I was powerless.

On St. Patrick's Day, a day of absolutely no significance in El Paso, I walked into the warehouse armed with a sack of freshly baked chocolate-chip cookies "from Beckworth". I asked the hack on duty to check the shoe inventory to see if he could find a size 12. Miraculously, he did! When I took off my clunkers and handed them to him—along with the cookies—I could see that I had walked through four layers of rubber. It had taken more than fourteen months to get a pair of shoes the right size.

A sack of baked goods had finally done the trick.

On March 30, after two winters working in our cramped, cold food-service office, our new office in the newly remodeled and expanded kitchen was ready for move-in. By camp standards, we had relocated "uptown" to a comfortable, heated and air-conditioned space with glass windows into the work areas.

One April morning, the PA system directed every inmate to move to the baseball field—except food-service inmates. Instead, we were directed to the perimeter fence behind the kitchen near the dumpster. As I turned at the bottom of the ramp toward the fence, I saw a sight that resembled a more sinister version of the Westminster Dog Show. Milling about were "America's finest" with their German Shepherd police dogs. It was drug-sniffing time at the country club!

The dog and handler teams had come from the U.S. Army and La Migra (U.S. Border Patrol)—the most, or least, popular government agency in these parts, depending on which side of the camp fence you lived on.

Cook Foreman Soto stood in front of our group of forty-three inmates to make sure no one bolted over the fence or made a mad dash back inside to hide something from the keen noses of the drug dogs. Just before the sniffing began, the faithful old garbage truck drove in to unload our dumpster. The food-service inmates let out a cheer for its timely arrival while the hacks frantically waved the driver off, fearing the truck might confuse the dogs.

Also in April, the warden reviewed the reports from locker searches done randomly throughout the camp. From his review, he realized that everyone stashed a roll of toilet paper in his locker. Since the inmates didn't have access to paper napkins, they all kept a half a roll of toilet paper to clean up after late evening meals. The warden concluded, however, that we were stealing toilet paper. He therefore removed the toilet paper from all bathrooms in Hueco and locked them up in the hack's office. Every time we needed toilet paper, we had to get a hack to unlock his office, unlock a cabinet, and then hand us the toilet paper. He'd then wait until we returned it so he could lock it back up—yet another example of "country club" living.

On April 29, Ms. Storey called me to her office. As I entered she said, "I just knew you would get 90 days of halfway-house time, but guess what? You only got thirty."

Her statement caught me off-guard. "What? Only thirty days? Ms. Storey, what have I done wrong? Nobody gets that few days unless they've been given shots or sent to the Hole."

"Well, that's all the warden would give you. No reason, but that's it. August 31."

I said nothing more, but I was furious. I turned abruptly and walked back to my room. Santa Anna—what an SOB! I guess he figured he couldn't keep me until my mandatory release date, so he gave me the next least amount. What a jerk! Was it my supposed "Harvard pedigree," my financially successful past, my cop-out request? It seemed to me that for no logical reason, he clearly had it in for me.

Around June 3, 1993, I was called to pick up a piece of "legal mail," which is from a lawyer or a court. The letter was from the U.S. Attorney's Office in Houston advising me that I would be coming to Houston to meet with them on a legal furlough.

I wasn't sure why they wanted me to come. Mary didn't know anything about it, either. I told Beckworth and Robles the situation, then found a replacement to do my work for the week I would be gone.

I could hardly contain my excitement when Mary told me on Wednesday, June 9, that she had talked with Doug Durham, the assistant U.S. attorney handling my case, and that I was to be released to her at 8 a.m. Sunday morning to bring me to Houston for a week—all according to a court order signed by Judge Hittner.

The following night, Mary told me that Doug had called the camp and talked with one of the assistant wardens. He'd been told that the camp would not release any inmate to anyone except the U.S. Marshals. That infuriated Doug, so he reminded the assistant warden that the document he'd faxed to her was a court order signed by a federal judge.

The assistant warden wouldn't give in. Doug exploded and told her that if I was not in the U.S. Attorney's office in Houston Monday morning at 9 a.m., the U.S. Marshals would be at the camp that afternoon to pick up the warden and bring him to Houston for a contempt-of-court hearing. He would personally have to explain to the judge why he disobeyed his order.

Begrudgingly, the assistant warden assured Doug that I would be released to Mary on Sunday.

When I took the flight schedule to Ms. Storey's office Friday morning to schedule my departure, she noted that our flight back to Houston didn't leave El Paso until noon, four hours after I had been released to Mary. Camp rules stated that an inmate could not leave the camp more than two hours before his time of departure from El Paso. Hence, I wouldn't be released until 10 a.m. I reported this to Mary, who immediately phoned Doug. He called the camp once more to make sure the BOP staff understood that all provisions of the order were to be obeyed. Again reluctantly, they agreed. On Sunday morning, I stood at the guardhouse ready to be released into Mary's custody at 8 a.m., and was without further incident.

It felt like a small "victory" in the face of the often merciless world of federal prison camp.

Almost 10 months after our wedding, Mary and I finally had a short furlough "honeymoon" in El Paso, then a wonderful longer one in Houston, though I did spend four days in the U.S. Attorney's office. I returned alone to the camp at 8 p.m. the following Sunday, thanks to Betty's driving me from the airport back to the camp. Before being released to my room, I was given urine and Breathalyzer tests, then strip-searched. Knowing these would be administered upon my return, and not having a substance-abuse problem, I avoided the only real risk—eating something containing poppy seeds, which show up in a drug test as though you had smoked marijuana.

Walking back to my room, all I could think about was that I had only sixty-six more days at FPC ELP. For almost a week, I had tasted a fairly normal life with Mary as "newlyweds." I had seen my family. I had smelled the fresh, exhilarating air of freedom. I wasn't out yet, but when I looked up now and saw that Southwest Airlines plane, I knew that one day soon I would be on it—traveling home to stay.

The day Mary dropped me off at the airport to return to El Paso, she learned that her mother was gravely ill. She flew to Milwaukee the next morning, but it meant several connecting flights. Due to delays and cancellations, a flight scheduled for three hours lasted twelve. With each passing hour, Mary became more frantic about getting to Milwaukee with enough time to say goodbye to her mother. Fortunately, she made it.

On June 28, Irene died from leukemia. Mary and I were grateful that she was able to spend those last days at Irene's bedside. And I shared Mary's grief. No one had ever accepted me so fully, unconditionally and quickly as Irene and Weston Jensen. It was a deep loss.

With the inmate population increasing to 500, our food-service staff had grown to almost 60 inmate employees. The volume of paperwork had grown with it. I could still get all of my work done each day, but I knew a replacement would soon be needed. I recommended Tim from Houston, who worked with Curtis at the warehouse. Tim joined us in mid-July to begin training. Now, it was really beginning to feel like this ordeal was coming to an end.

Shortly thereafter, I got a letter from L. D. Blackwell saying that I had a job with his company as soon as I got back to Houston. What a friend—and what a relief! Having a job meant I could go home every weekend from the halfway house. Things were looking up.

The letters that I mailed to Mary every night were actually a "journal" which she then copied and mailed to my family. I wanted to use that material to write about this experience after my release. To encourage my effort, Barry, a practicing architect, and also an adjunct professor at the University of Houston's Graduate School of Architecture, offered to enroll me in its Creative Writing School for the fall semester. But the semester started before August 31. I filed another cop-out asking for a transfer to the half-way house a few days earlier than August 31 to give me time to register. Based on recent history, I wasn't optimistic that it would be granted.

Before my request was answered, I received a letter from New Directions, the federal halfway house in Houston, advising me that I would be reporting August 26. I had to read it twice before believing it was true. Santa Anna had granted my last request. I was almost out of here!

On August 21, Mary told me that Marian's boyfriend, Chris Casey, wanted me to call him. I made the collect call, and Chris immediately asked if he could marry my daughter—exactly what I'd been hoping. They had known each other all of their lives because of the closeness of our families. That connection had grown into infatuation and then love over the years.

Letting out a whoop when he asked, I replied with a hearty "YES!" I felt thrilled for Marian and Chris, but at the same time saddened that he had to accept a collect call from me in prison to pose the question. Another bittersweet moment.

On Sunday morning, August 22, the chaplain asked me to speak at the Sunday service—a tradition when an inmate was scheduled to leave the camp the following week. I used the opportunity to introduce an excerpt from Les Miserables by

Victor Hugo to my audience of about thirty inmates. I wanted to illustrate that we were all here for many different reasons, some right and some wrong. But being here, we needed to focus on the future, not on the past, just as Jean Valjean had done in Hugo's inspirational story.

Then, using as an example the death of Lazarus from John 11 in the Bible, I said that even though the punishment sometimes seems to never stop coming, or feels overly harsh, perhaps that's because, like Lazarus, we must die—reaching the very end of ourselves and our strength—before we can be raised again.

Monday, August 23 was Mary's and my first wedding anniversary. I spent most of the day arranging to have my things mailed home, then excitedly called Mary to express my love for her, for the trials and tribulations she had endured for my sake and to share the joy of my coming home and building our new life together.

The next day was my last at FPC, and my 56th birthday. I spent the entire day collecting all seven BOP department heads' signatures on a form. I would have to go from building to building to find them, and if they were out or tied up, I would have to return. That's why the inmates called this "merry-go-round" day.

There were several department heads I had grown to like and respect, such as Beckworth, and it was emotional for me to say goodbye. With the pent-up excitement of finally leaving El Paso for Houston, it took quite a while to fall asleep that night.

But I knew that in the morning, I would leave this camp for good as a free man.

Twelve

D (DEPARTURE) DAY
August 25, 1993

When I awoke, it was my 601st day, but the time had seemed like an eternity. I was finally going home, and no one could prevent it. I ate breakfast with a couple of friends, then leisurely walked to the R&D building. No longer was R&D in a trailer; it was now part of a newly renovated building. As my bus to Houston was not scheduled to leave El Paso until 11:30, the camp would not release me before 9:30.

From there I walked to the cashier's office in the main building, where I was given a prison voucher to be redeemed at the El Paso bus station for a ticket. The camp gave me $50 (a gift to all departing inmates), cash for a meal, taxi fare to the halfway house, the balance in my commissary account ($280.92) and my driver's license. Then I signed final documents evidencing my departure.

Inmate Jose's job was to drive discharged inmates to the bus station. As I was the only one leaving that morning, he grabbed my small bag and put it in the van. We climbed into the front seats.

He cranked up the van. "Congratulations on going home. You got a job when you get there?"

"Yeah, sure do. I'm pretty lucky. A friend is helping me out."

"Well, you won't have to put up with all this bullshit anymore!"

"No, and I'm grateful for that. It's no country club, is it, Jose?"

"Country club, my ass," he smiled. "Whoever says that should be an inmate for a while. It's the sh--s, staff always f---ing with your head, changing the rules."

I certainly couldn't argue the point. "Well, you hang in there, 'cause you'll be going home soon," I offered.

"Yeah, I'll be down three more months, then I'm getting the hell out of here, too."

He drove slowly out of the parking lot and toward the prison entrance. At the guardhouse, Jose stopped. The hack— a likeable guy named Castaneda—came out to check our paperwork. He approved everything, shook my hand, and wished me well. Until yesterday during my "merry-go-round," no FPC staff member had ever shaken my hand—another BOP rule.

As the van crept out onto the open road past the cyclone fence, my eyes filled rapidly with tears. I quickly turned to my right so Jose wouldn't see them. I pretended to look at the Franklin mountains in the distance. As he drove slowly, I watched with blurred vision as the rolling hills of Fort Bliss rose and fell with the van. I thanked God for giving me all I had needed to get through this experience. But I was also a little sad to leave the friends I had made.

During this emotion-packed, twenty-minute ride in the prison's white van to the El Paso bus station, it gradually sunk in. I was finally out of prison.

It was not just another day. It was August 25, 1993, my "D" day. I was on the way home. Tears of joy rolled down my cheeks like an eighteen-wheeler headed downhill on an open road, toward an ever-brightening horizon.

Thirteen

New Directions

At the bus station, I exchanged the prison-issued voucher for a ticket that would have bought me a grueling, 12-hour bus trip to Houston, via Dallas. Like most inmates, I couldn't wait to get home, and even though it violated camp rules, many flew home instead. Shoving the bus ticket in my pocket, I walked quickly outside where Betty was waiting to drive me to the El Paso airport, where I would finally board that familiar orange Southwest Airlines plane to freedom that I had dreamed about for the past twenty months.

I felt squeamish violating the rule, like I had more than four decades earlier when I snuck out of Lanier Junior High School at lunch time with a friend to see a movie. I wouldn't feel safe until I was seated on the plane and it was taxiing down the runway. My heart was pounding as I walked through the airport and boarded the jet. As it hurtled down the runway and lifted off, I said a prayer of thanks. Looking out the window, I could see FPC ELP fade into the distance. I was finally on my way.

Mary was anxiously waiting for me as I stepped off the plane (in the now-bygone era of airport reunions at the gate). The moment she saw me, she ran into my arms in a tender, tearful embrace that seemed to last several minutes. There are no words to describe how I felt at that moment.

Arriving in Seabrook, the fresh breeze with the slight smell of salt water instantly reminded me of why I had felt so strongly about living here. Just walking down to the bulkhead, watching and hearing the bay water ebb and flow, was therapeutic. I savored the moment. That evening, Mary and I sat on our porch watching seagulls fly in front of the houses along the bay, and a few sailboats come in from an afternoon of fun. As I closed my eyes, it felt almost like being at a tropical resort.

I was uncertain about what my thirty-five days at New Directions halfway house would be like. I knew that Buddy would be there, but I probably wouldn't know anyone else because they would be coming from different federal prisons. From my experience at FPC ELP, I knew that most would also be completing sentences for some kind of a drug conviction.

As I arrived just before 7 a.m. on August 26, many of the inmates were leaving for work. I checked in, was assigned a room and finished the paperwork. Since I had a job and auto insurance, I was permitted to drive my old, well-worn '82 Chevy Suburban to work and go home on the weekends. Located in a rundown area on the north side of Houston, ND was an older apartment project that had been refurbished and completely enclosed by a tall, cyclone fence. It had two wings, one for federal and the other for state inmates. In our wing, two inmates were assigned to each room and shared a bathroom with the adjoining room. It resembled a college dormitory "suite". There were several large common areas that were carpeted and furnished with sofas and overstuffed arm chairs for watching TV, visiting or reading. Compared to FPC ELP, it was a Five Star Hotel.

At Blackwell Plastics Inc., I collected delinquent accounts receivable and was paid $1,000 per month. I had hoped to return to my consulting position with Village Title Company, but Village was in the process of being closed. However, I was grateful for the job I had and the privileges it permitted.

Every Friday when I was paid, I had to buy a money order for 25 percent of that amount and drive back across Houston in often gridlocked Friday-afternoon traffic to give it to New Directions. Then I was free to drive home for the weekend. The whole procedure was a hassle, but a small price to pay to be back home with Mary.

Breakfast and dinner at ND were served cafeteria-style in a common dining hall. The food was more varied than at the camp, and seconds and thirds were allowed. Before leaving for my job, I made a sack lunch by selecting from a variety of lunch meats and bread, chips, fruit and cookies—and I could make it as big as my appetite.

When I returned from my first day at work and walked through the TV area, Buddy was sitting there. Better dressed than almost everyone at ND, he wore slacks, a starched dress shirt and polished loafers. He looked like I remembered him when he relaxed at River Oaks Country Club, except that he had lost some weight. That was likely a product of his giving up his daily cocktails for almost two years. We greeted each other cordially, and he suggested eating supper together. During the meal, he said his warden had given him sixty days in the halfway house.

During our conversation, he admitted, "We did the right thing by pleading guilty."

I looked for clues in his expression, but it was without emotion. It was just a pragmatic statement. At his prison camp in Texarkana, he had learned what happened to those who went to trial and lost: They got much longer sentences.

"Yeah," I smiled, "we sure got back home a lot sooner than those guys!"

The next evening as I came out of the cafeteria, I passed one of the counselors. We greeted each other and I added how good and plentiful the food was. He nodded, smiled and asked me where I'd been. When I said FPC ELP, he responded, "That's a hell hole."

How interesting, I thought. Perhaps I can explore that later.

I don't recall seeing Buddy again at ND. Having arrived a month earlier than I, he had the right to eat dinner at home every night after he got off work and report in later.

The Friday night of my first weekend at home, Mary and I celebrated by eating dinner at our favorite romantic restaurant, and then drove around Seabrook noting the changes that occurred over the past twenty months. We returned home very tired, fell in bed and held each other tightly as our problems melted away. We were soon fast asleep.

About 10:30 p.m., I bolted upright in bed screaming, "Oh no! I forgot to call New Directions!"

I was required to call by 10 p.m. every night to let them know I was home. Mary leaped out of bed and began searching for the number. What would my punishment be—maybe no more nights at home? I wasn't up to anything wrong, but I hadn't followed the rule. I said a quick prayer, "Please God, help me find that number so I can call in before it gets any later."

I joined Mary in searching for the phone number, found one, and hastily dialed it. No answer. My heart sank; it was the daytime number. What did I do with that other number? I sifted through papers on the kitchen counter as my anxiety level ratcheted up with each passing moment. Finally, I found another number and dialed it. A male voice calmly answered, "New Directions."

I exhaled and haltingly explained who I was, my inmate number, that I fell asleep before 10 and forgot to call, but I was home and he could talk to my wife to prove it...

He was chuckling. "Don't worry, Bro. I got ya covered."

Instantly relieved, my throbbing heart slowly returned to its normal rate, but it took quite awhile to wind down and go back to sleep.

The next morning, looking at unpacked boxes and furniture stacked everywhere, it was hard to know where to begin. I decided that since the grass needed to be cut, I had a good excuse to get my old John Deere garden mower out. The smell of freshly cut grass and the view of the bay made even the most mundane chore a pleasure.

On September 29, I was processed by the Probation Department and assigned to a U.S. probation officer. When I left New Directions the morning of the 30th, I was no longer incarcerated. My sentence had been served, but I still had three years ahead of me of supervised release.

And what a mountain of challenges I faced: I had to get a full-time job with a decent salary and benefits. Mary was now collecting unemployment compensation because the home-building company she had been working for had transferred her to a subdivision in another town on the far side of Houston. She had pleaded with them to reassign her closer to home, because it was much too far to commute, but to no avail. It was a relief to know that she would be receiving at least some income for a few months while we both continued our job search.

Now that I was back home, I also had to get back into the bankruptcy case to obtain a discharge and, simultaneously, argue with the IRS that I didn't owe any additional taxes. I had more to do now than before I had left for FPC ELP—but with only a fraction of the income. The difficulties seemed unending and almost insurmountable. I had to keep reminding myself that I couldn't solve all of the problems at once. All I could do was deal with them one at a time.

In determining the restitution that Buddy and I each owed the RTC, Judge Hittner had taken the money involved in the three criminal transactions and divided it in half, which was $573,925.83. It wasn't completely fair since Buddy had gotten $175,000 of the first $185,000, but that was only a minor irritant. My major question now was whether the U.S. Attorney and Judge Hittner would consider the $500,000 paid to the RTC in settlement of my bankruptcy-fraud case—which was based primarily on those same three transactions— as satisfactory restitution in my criminal case. My attorneys, Raymond Kerr and Bill Burge, thought it should be. I was concerned, though, because to argue that position, I would incur more legal fees.

At one of the first meetings with my probation officer, he said he had looked over my entire file and thought that my restitution had been paid. He said he would verify that with the U.S. Attorney's office. I was flabbergasted. Immediately my hopes escalated through the roof that I wouldn't owe any more restitution, or incur any additional legal fees. Could I be so fortunate?

Several months later, the U.S. Attorney's office agreed that the half-million-dollar settlement paid in the bankruptcy case would also apply to the criminal case! It filed a motion with the court reflecting that I had satisfied the restitution requirement, and Judge Hittner signed the order. The big contingency had been eliminated. I was relieved, but I still had no full-time job, had to repay Jerrol Springer for our mortgage payments, and faced ongoing legal and accounting fees.

Aside from having to turn in a written report each month when I met with my probation officer, I had a new set of rules to follow. For one, I could not drive 65 miles northwest of Houston to see my parents, who lived just outside the Southern District of Texas, without written consent. On my first visit to see them, I made sure that I did not exceed the speed limit. I was anxious because if I was stopped, the officer would check my driver's license and learn that I was a felon on supervised release. Then what would happen? For my own peace of mind, for three years I always drove under the speed limit!

*"While we don't get to choose
the result of our choice,
we do get to choose
how we respond to the result."*

– HARVIN C. MOORE III

Fourteen

Struggling to Find a Purpose

I never could have imagined how hard it was to find a permanent job. My sentence prohibited me for three years from holding a job with a financial institution that involved a fiduciary responsibility, and I had lost my law license. So I focused on finding a job in real-estate development or homebuilding.

I was well-known in the community and experienced in a number of areas. I just needed a job. Whether I asked friends, or they referred me to someone else, the answer always was the same: no one was hiring, or no one wanted to hire a convicted felon. The pain of rejection stung more deeply with each one. Because I had owned my own businesses for quite a while, some employers thought it might be hard to have someone else setting my agenda. I knew that would not be a problem, having lived through prison. Others seemed leery that I would either revert to being the "boss" or be unhappy that I was not. Given the opportunity, I knew I could disprove those assumptions.

It made me angry, but I would not let that show. I tried to avoid negative situations because I didn't want to be dragged down emotionally any further, but some were unavoidable.

With Mary's encouragement and reassurance each evening, I would make it through this difficult time.

On a much happier note, it was now time for the "wedding blessing" that Mary and I had planned when we had exchanged vows at FPC ELP. On March 26, 1994, in a part of our yard that faced Galveston Bay, we held the ceremony for our families and friends. Mary's sister, Nancy, and her brother-in-law, Tony, came from Minneapolis, while her father came from Milwaukee. He stayed with us for a month, which became an annual vacation for him. My entire family attended along with our friends. It was a postcard-perfect day except for the high winds, so gusty that we had to move the blessing away from the bay shore. Mary ordered a special cake—no honey buns this time. The day holds many cherished memories, including Tony and me spending the morning putting fire-ant poison on all the mounds in the yard while Mary and Nancy worked in the house preparing for the party.

The Saturday after our wedding blessing, I got a frantic phone call. Daddy had experienced a cardiac arrest and had died suddenly in Chappell Hill, less than two months before his eighty-ninth birthday.

He had gotten critically ill several times while I was in prison, but had pulled through. I will always believe that my dad willed himself to live until I got home. That, too, was a blessing, yet I knew I would miss his dry sense of humor and self-deprecating wit which had helped me so much in navigating the last five years. It was his finest chapter in being my father.

In February, I had been interviewed for a job with Housing Opportunities of Houston Inc. (HOH), a nonprofit organization that assisted first-time homebuyers with educational and training programs. HOH had been given some foreclosed houses by the FDIC and RTC, which it refurbished and sold. Needing someone to manage its housing venture, HOH hired me in March but did not give a start date because it had to determine how it would fund the position. However, the mere news that I had a job had sent a wave of excitement through our families. At last, Mary and I were hopeful that with a regular income we could manage our financial obligations. But HOH could not decide on the day for me to begin, and I became more frustrated with each passing week. Finally in May, I had had enough. I told HOH I was showing up for work and expected to be paid.

Once I started, each workday was a joy. I was doing something I knew how to do and believed in its mission. More important, it gave me a tremendous boost in confidence because not only did HOH know about my conviction, but I was replacing someone who had stolen tens of thousands of dollars from its housing venture.

Over the summer and fall, we finished and sold some houses, meeting the schedule and budgets we had agreed upon. By the end of the year, however, HOH was experiencing management problems and tension at the board level. Steve Bancroft, rector of Trinity Episcopal Church in Houston and founder of HOH, was chairman emeritus of the board's executive committee of the board. He and John Hernandez, the chairman, asked me if I would consider becoming interim president of HOH if the current one was removed. I agreed, provided HOH would put my name on the list for consideration in its search for the eventual president.

Several months later, the president was removed, and I was nominated by the executive committee for the interim post. I was not present at the board meeting but was told by the chairman the next morning that a disgruntled board member (a close friend of the deposed president) had threatened to call the Houston Chronicle if I were chosen, and tell them that HOH had selected a convicted felon as its president. With that, my nomination was withdrawn and the board hired a consulting firm to run the organization.

Worse still, they could only pay my salary for 30 more days. It was devastating. What would I do now? In less than a year, I had lost a job I loved and instantly was thrown back into the job market. I was demoralized.

With no job prospects and bills beginning to pile up, we were getting desperate. I had to do something and quickly. Mary and I believed in the mission of helping to provide housing for low-income, first-time homebuyers. So we decided to form a small remodeling company, Renewed Housing Corporation, and solicit work from other nonprofits. Ed Saconas, a friend since law school, gave me the opportunity to bid on some work that he managed for a nonprofit. I knew the subs to use since they had been working for me on HOH jobs, but now I had full construction responsibility which, in this niche, meant doing some of the work myself. I threw myself into it, and Mary joined with me to make deadlines, select materials and complete other tasks.

Despite remodeling a number of houses over the next year, our effort seemed futile because we hadn't made a profit. We decided that if we remodeled a more expensive house, we would have better margins and could make a reasonable profit.

With the confidence of my banker friend, Frank Hathorn, who agreed to make us a construction loan, we bought an old house in the Houston Heights area to remodel. We both enjoyed the work; Mary was especially talented in interior design. It took us about nine months to complete, and we expected to sell it quickly and make a nice profit.

Unfortunately, it didn't sell, even though we followed our realtor's advice and dropped the price several times. Mary was convinced that it was a realtor problem, not a house or pricing problem. She finally persuaded me to change agencies. Our new realtor advised us that once we had lowered the sales price, we could not raise it. Within two months, our new realtor had sold the house, but, once again, we had not made a profit.

We continued to have no income but, thank goodness, with credit cards we could buy what we needed, including groceries. I was desperate and still looking feverishly for a job.

A few months later, a friend recommended me to Jim Perryman, who owned Phase One Technologies, an environmental-site assessment firm. Jim needed someone to market his company. Though it was a full-commission job, I accepted it in the fall of '96.

This was a new field for me. I immersed myself in learning the technical aspects of environmental assessment and the nuances of how it applied to real-estate ownership and development. Phase One was a small company with a family feel. I was optimistic that I could bring in new business, but I needed to do it quickly.

We were falling further and further in debt. Would I have to file bankruptcy again? Something good needed to happen soon.

My tax case had evolved into one overriding issue: whether I had a personal net operating loss to carry forward, or just a capital loss to carry forward. If I won the point, all my future income would be tax-sheltered for years. Otherwise, only my gains from the sale of investments would be sheltered (assuming I had any future gains).

In December, Raymond Kerr called with the news that the IRS had finally agreed to accept all of the points we had made if we agreed to its major issue: that my losses were capital and not net operating. By agreeing, I would have paid more taxes than I owed and would receive a refund, almost $100,000.

Had I just heard that correctly—the IRS owed me money?

I stammered, "I don't understand. All I wanted was to end up not owing the IRS one more dollar, but you're telling me it owes me money? I don't believe it!"

"It's true," he confirmed. "I'll fax you the settlement docs for you to study, and we'll talk tomorrow. In the meantime, I'll tell the IRS to calculate the exact amount."

I put the phone down in a daze. After seven long years and an expensive battle, the IRS owed me money. I felt vindicated. The capital-loss carry forward would do me no good except to provide an ordinary income-tax deduction of $3,000 per year. At that rate, it would take more than 300 years to use it up…slightly more than my life expectancy. But I could live with that. The refund—it was like manna from heaven. I felt like David must have felt when Goliath went down.

With the refund I could pay my legal and accounting fees and some other bills, with a little left over. It was the best news I had heard in a number of years. This unforeseen development, coupled with a new job, brought on a sense of euphoria.

That evening, as Mary and I sat on our porch watching the sailboats returning to their marinas, with their sails reflecting the golden glow of the setting sun, it seemed like things had finally turned for us—upward, this time.

Jerre Frazier, a lawyer from Houston whom I had known for years, called from Nashville to extend an invitation. He had recently become the Director of Compliance for Columbia/ HCA, then the nation's largest health care provider, and asked me to be the "ethics" speaker at its day-and-a-half seminar during the annual meeting of its executives in Washington, D.C. in March 1997. He felt that hearing about my experience would be more meaningful than a dry, legalistic ethics lecture.

I was thrilled to be asked and eagerly accepted, particularly when he said that the company wanted both Mary and me to come for the full, four-day meeting. She shared my enthusiasm and looked forward to a much-needed vacation.

While I had talked to "at-risk" high school students in the Houston Independent School District after I returned from El Paso, it was during a talk I gave to an ethics class at the University of Houston Law Center in 1995 that I realized the keen interest I could engender in an audience about "doing the right thing" by relating my experiences. Now I had the opportunity to deliver that message to a group of fifteen hundred executives. It was also apparent that federal investigations were beginning in the health care field. As an executive who had lived through the S&L failures, I could prepare them for what might lie ahead.

I organized my thoughts and began researching fraud and abuse issues in health care to understand the pressures and temptations that my audience faced every day. I felt that I had to get them to absorb my experience to better understand the risks and feel the pain of giving in. I wanted them to grasp the rationalizations that often "justify" wrong choices. If I could do that powerfully, I might earn other opportunities to share my story.

The evening before my program, I felt that I was as ready as I would ever be, except that I needed a powerful closing. At around 4 a.m., I awoke and, in order not to disturb Mary, went into the bathroom to read my daily devotional. As I opened the Bible, there was Jeremiah 31:33, where the Lord said, "I will put my law in their minds and will write it on their hearts..." I realized that was our moral compass, and that we all have it. We just need to look within to find and follow it.

Within minutes after taking the podium, I spoke of my wrong choices and the agony and pain they had caused. My inner most thoughts and feelings flowed forth. The ballroom was silent. Not one person left the room; they were spellbound.

You could hear a pin drop on the carpet.

As I looked at the audience, I knew that my message was resonating with them and could change people's lives. This was my true calling, and I was ready to embrace it.

Epilogue

Now, after a long and, at times, seemingly endless struggle, my life is better than I could have ever imagined.

Within a week after I had spoken at the Columbia/HCA annual executives meeting, I received the refund from the IRS. Holding that check in my hand represented the conclusion of an entire decade of the legal battles I had endured.

Over the following months, it became apparent that I could not generate enough income working for Phase One. I found myself searching for a job once again, and wondering if I would ever find work that would provide a future for Mary and me.

Just when everything seemed hopeless, Walter Jefferson, an attorney in Houston I had known for many years, hired me as a legal assistant. Working with Walter provided the base from which I was reacquainted with the legal practice, and I could finally envision a future. For the next two and one-half years I loved what I was doing, but yearned to get my law license back.

Five years after completing my sentence, I excitedly walked into the Harris County Clerk's Office and registered to vote. I was surprised at how much I had missed that basic

American right and vowed never to miss the opportunity to cast a ballot.

With the confidence from working with Walter and encouragement from a number of lawyer friends, I applied for reinstatement to the State Bar of Texas. Our state law requires a non-jury trial in a district court to determine the suitability of the applicant to be readmitted. The State Bar, as a matter of policy, contests every Motion for Reinstatement; thus, it's an adversarial proceeding.

In support of my Motion, I called as witnesses one banker, Frank N. Hathorn, and six attorneys: Charles R. "Bob" Dunn, Walter Jefferson, Raymond C. Kerr, Robert P. "Bob" Schuwerk, Jack M. Webb and Michael E. Clark. Mike, the former head of the Financial Fraud Section of the U.S. Attorney's Office for the Southern District of Texas, had prosecuted me. I was overcome with emotion as he explained to the Court that it was my honesty and integrity that he witnessed during my criminal case that led him to testify in my behalf.

At the conclusion of the trial in June 1999, the Judge granted my Motion, subject to passing the bar exam within eighteen months.

My excitement quickly dissipated, however, as I realized that thirty-seven years after taking that three-day exam the first time, I would have to learn almost an entire body of new law and how the courts interpreted it. Studying was a long and grueling process. The test itself left me physically and mentally spent. But in November 2000 in Austin, I was sworn in as a "new" lawyer. I had come full circle. My personal reha-bilitation was complete.

About the same time, a long-time friend, Jim Lindsey, a mortgage banker in Houston, approached me about doing real-estate development with him. I had avoided that business because I feared no one would be my partner, nor would any lender want a project of mine in its portfolio. Jim felt that, with full disclosure, it would not be an issue. We formed Lindsey & Moore Investment, LLC, a small real-estate development company with no employees. I was once again drawn into real-estate development, but this time, without any financial liability and with a partner with whom I share completely mutual values. As a result, we have absolute confidence and trust in each other. It has been a pleasure to work together, combining our expertise in planning and building subdivisions in Houston.

Jon Pollock, a Houston business owner and speaker for TEC (The Executive Committee, now Vistage, the world's largest CEO-membership organization), had seen Columbia/HCA's video of my presentation. Believing it could be expanded into a program for TEC's members, introduced me to Steve Brody, a highly regarded TEC Chair in Houston. With Steve's guidance, I developed a corporate-training program, *Seven Steps for Ethical Growth©*, to build on my personal experience, and presented it the first time to Steve's CEO group the morning of September 11, 2001. My nervousness that morning quickly evaporated when a member arrived with the news of the terrorist attack on the World Trade Center buildings in New York City. A TV was turned on and my presentation interrupted about every half-hour for an update. Somehow I managed to get through that morning. I gave two more programs for Steve's other groups later that week, then waited on whether other TEC chapters would want my program. After several months, the calls began to come in. As I look back over the past eight and one-half years, I am astounded that I have presented almost 400 programs to its chapters throughout the United States, Canada and the United Kingdom, and been rated among its Top Ten speakers.

A frequent keynote speaker at conferences, conventions, corporate meetings, universities and religious meetings, I tell my story in a dramatic and memorable way. I emphasize the fact that I did not have the courage to make the right Choice. The Choice I made caused tremendous pain and embarrassment not only to me, but more important, to the people around me. I paid a horrendous price for making that choice, and it changed my life forever.

It was a tedious and extended battle to recover and build a new life. I never gave up, though there were times when I didn't think I had the strength to go on. But with faith and occasionally unexpected good news, I would be given renewed hope. As I look back over my experience, I feel like I am called to bring my message of hope and redemption to you.

If, through my example, I can give you the strength to persevere in hard times and inspire you to summon the courage to make the right choice, whether in business or in other areas of your life, my journey will have been worthwhile, because then you will be able to say:

"One Choice Changed My Life—For The Better."

Author's Note

If my story has touched your life and empowered you to make the right choice, or if you felt hopeless, but now have renewed hope, please write and tell me how *"One Choice Can Change Your Life"* has changed your life.

Email Harvin at:
onechoicecanchangeyourlife@gmail.com

Acknowledgments

This book has been a multi-year project and I could not have completed it without the patience, understanding and support of my wife, Mary. She not only provided significant creative input, but also monitored every detail in bringing *One Choice Can Change Your Life* to print. Along the way, she single-handledly forced me to move beyond the impersonal narration of facts and delve into the underlying emotions I felt as I lived these chapters.

My brother, Barry Moore, has been a constant, nurturing supporter of my writing. Jim Robinson, a professor at the University of Houston's Creative Writing School, urged me to write my story as non-fiction rather than hide behind fictionalizing it. He firmly believed that if it were written honestly and with emotion, it would be more powerful.

As I began speaking about my experiences, Tracy Sherba, office coordinator for The Executive Committee (TEC) of Canada, Ltd., became an early advocate of my presentations and insisted that I write about my journey. Persistently, but gently, she kept me working toward that goal.

Tim Fields of Fields Publishing Company spurred me to write it all down with abandon; then, and only then, edit it.

But the focus of the book was not clearly defined until our marketing consultant, James Malinchak, identified its primary market as business leaders and came up with the title.

Upon completion of an updated manuscript, Yvette Womack provided the honest and unbiased opinion of a typical reader. With revisions made, Michael E. Clark, an attorney in Houston and the former Assistant U.S. Attorney who oversaw my prosecution, cast his critical eye on the text from an entirely different perspective, which was invaluable.

Just before publication, Dan Fisher, a Senior Editor at *Forbes*, in spite of his own formidable deadlines, found time to read the manuscript and offer his valuable suggestions.

The final edit was performed by Phil Newman, of NewManifest Communications who was able to streamline and tighten without changing the tenor of my words and thoughts. His daily newspaper background enabled him to respond within tight deadlines as well. It was a joy to work with Phil.

Troy Birdsong of Birdsong Creative designed the covers, and his creative genius enabled us to present the book, including its formatting, in the most appealing way. He, too, captured the essence of the message of the book and took our ideas to a higher level.

I am extremely grateful for the time and encouragement that each of these family, friends, and business leaders unselfishly gave to enable me to bring this book to fruition.

CPSIA information can be obtained at www.ICGtesting.com
Printed in the USA
LVOW06s0701120514

385359LV00002B/6/P